THE ULTIMATE NURSE
ACTIVITY BOOK

Claire Meloni

ISBN: 978-1-64845-107-2

CONTENTS

INTRODUCTION

Surely there are few jobs more rewarding, more necessary, and more important than nursing.

Nurses help us at the hardest and sometimes the lowest points of our life, and are always these with much-needed care, advice, and—sometimes more important than anything else—a reassuring smile.

But as important a job as nursing is, it's also one of the toughest. Years of intense studying and training are followed by long hours and even longer days on hospital wards, which can often prove as emotionally demanding as they are physically and mentally exhausting.

Happily, though, that's precisely where this book comes in!

Specially compiled for the nurse in your life (or, if you're a nurse yourself, just for you!) this is **The Ultimate Nurse Activity Book**.

What follows is over 100 pages of games, puzzles, quizzes, jumbles, jokes, facts, fun, and did-you-knows, all intended to give you something to wind down with and take your mind off everything at the end of a long day.

So let's get started! Grab a pen, kick back and put your feet up, as we tackle puzzle number 1...

Here's a straightforward one to kick things off! Can you find all of these common reasons for visiting the emergency department in the grid below?

- [ ] ANIMAL BITE
- [ ] BROKEN BONE
- [ ] BRUISE
- [ ] BURNS
- [ ] CUTS
- [ ] FEVER

- [ ] FRACTURE
- [ ] LACERATION
- [ ] PUNCTURE WOUND
- [ ] SPRAIN
- [ ] STOMACH BUG
- [ ] TRIPS AND FALLS

```
U S F G C P E F I V V O E D U
D E R U T C A R F U C A N O T
E N O B N E K O R B B U N F R
D O K H H X I B I N O M R R I
S I J C K B P B A W T A Q F P
L T A A S G P P E C N L E W S
G A O M Q N O R E I N V X R A
K R O O J J U U M S E A Q X N
H E C T X T Q A N R I J O H D
J C B S C Z L R U I C U T S F
B A I N C B U N X M E P R G A
E L U I I B S P R A I N D B L
S P X T I A J A Y R V B A V L
C A E A F O Y J R X Z F D D S
X I B H H P N Z A Y G H S F R
```

All the items from a first aid kit listed below link together in the grid.

Can you find the right home for them all?

- ALCOHOL
- ANTISEPTIC WIPE
- BANDAGES
- CALAMINE
- COLD PACK
- COTTON WOOL
- EMERGENCY BLANKET
- GAUZE
- GLOVES
- HAND SANITIZER
- IODINE
- LOTION
- MASK
- SAFETY PIN
- SCISSORS
- SEWING NEEDLES
- SWABS
- SYRINGE
- TAPE
- THERMOMETER
- TWEEZERS

Time to kick back with a classic sudoku puzzle. To solve a sudoku grid, you need to fill in the numbers 1–9 in such a way that each row, each column, and each smaller set of 3 x 3 squares contain each number just once and once only. Given the numbers already entered into the grid below, can you complete the puzzle?

	6		4	5			3	8
4		3				5	7	
		8		3	2			
2			7	1	9		6	
6		4	5		3	9	8	
				8		1	2	5
3					5			2
		2					9	
				9			5	

Can you find your way through the maze and back to the nurse's station?

Here's a tricky logic puzzle to pit your wits against.

Five people—Mrs. Adams, Mr. Bryant, Mrs. Charles, Mr. Davison, and Mrs. Edmunds—have turned up at the emergency room. Each of them has suffered an accident at home: one of them has burnt their hand; someone has bumped their head; another has cut their finger; another has wrenched their shoulder; and someone else has grazed their knee.

Based only on the clues below, can you work out who has hurt what part of their body?

1. Mrs. Charles has not hurt her knee...

2. ...and Mrs. Edmunds has not bumped her head!

3. The man who cut his finger while cooking has a surname that comes alphabetically immediately after the lady who tripped and grazed her knee.

4. The person who has hurt their shoulder is a man.

PATIENT	INJURY
Mrs. Adams	
Mr. Bryant	
Mrs. Charles	
Mr. Davison	
Mrs. Edmunds	

Here's a tricky test of your observational skills... Take a look at the grid below.

Are there more pens, more clipboards, or more thermometers?

Here's a tricky word game for you. The answers to all the crossword-style clues below can be made from the letters of the word HOSPITAL. No letters are used more than once in each answer. Can you work out all ten clues?

HOSPITAL

1. To clean to a sheen (6)

   _____

2. Aviator (5)

   _____

3. Relating to the mail service (6)

   _____

4. Poignancy, a quality evoking sadness or pity (6)

   _____

5. Of a child, overindulged or mollycoddled (6)

   _____

6. End of the handle of a sword (4)

   _____

7. Paved outdoor area in a yard (5)

   _____

8. Small firearm (6)

   _____

9. Lift up, raise (5)

   _____

10. Pitch of singing voice between soprano and tenor (4)

    _____

Here's a fiendish game all about the human body. The names of 15 bodily organs are hidden in the grid below. Unlike in an ordinary wordsearch, though, they're not all in straight lines! Can you find all the answers, so that no letter is used in multiple words, and all 100 letters are used once with none left over? The first has been filled in for you to make a start.

S	T	O	M	A	N	I	X	L	L
P	A	A	R	C	T	E	N	A	U
C	N	I	B	H	T	S	Y	R	N
R	S	N	T	H	I	T	R	A	G
E	K	I	N	Y	N	G	H	E	S
A	T	O	N	R	E	A	L	L	B
S	E	U	G	O	I	D	M	G	L
E	N	K	Y	T	I	A	P	A	A
E	L	I	E	O	D	E	H	R	D
S	P	D	N	N	G	U	R	E	D

The names of TWO things a nurse might carry in their pocket—one a five letter word, the other an eleven letter word—have been jumbled together here. Can you pull them apart?

ACEEEHHMMORRTTTW

Can you unjumble today's lunch menu?

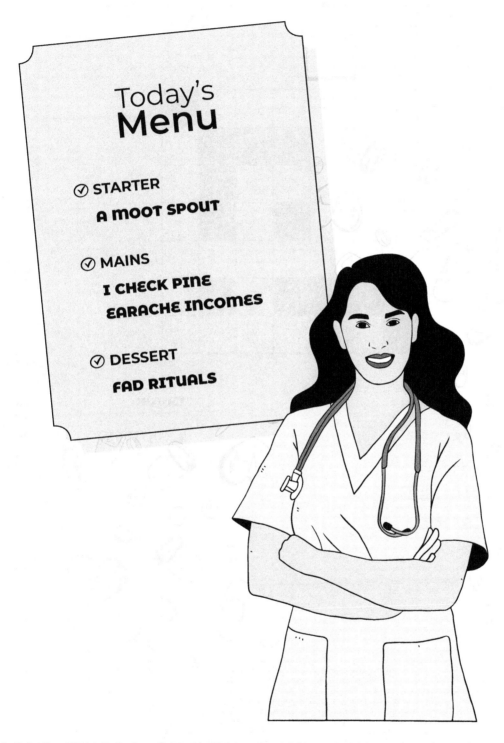

Today's
Menu

✓ STARTER
A MOOT SPOUT

✓ MAINS
**I CHECK PINE
EARACHE INCOMES**

✓ DESSERT
FAD RITUALS

NEVER TRUST A NURSE WHO SMILES WHEN SOMETHING GOES
WRONG...IT USUALLY MEANS SHE'S GOING OFF DUTY.

Here's a quick mini crossword—with a difference! All the answers are anagrams of the clue words. Unjumble each one to complete the grid.

Across

1. PARSES

4. STALK

6. HORSE

7. SPINET

Down

1. SAINTS

2. TALAS

3. PLEASE

5. PORTS

Solve this cryptogram to reveal a nursing one-liner!

" ___ __-_A_ _____ _M__T

"XC K-QVC VIIJNFTXAFT

__ ___ _OS_____

VT TRA RJOINTVE

_____K__E__ _____,

TJJL VZAO TJHVC,

_____ _Y__L__

GASVBOA TRAC JFEC

H___ __ _____ N___F_!"

RVH V OLAEATJF OTVDD!"

Can you find all of these different parts of a hospital in the grid below?

☐ CARDIOLOGY
☐ EMERGENCY / DEPARTMENT
☐ DIALYSIS
☐ DISPENSARY
☐ OUTPATIENTS
☐ PEDIATRIC CARE

☐ PHARMACY
☐ RECEPTION
☐ RECORDS
☐ SURGERY
☐ WARDS
☐ XRAY

```
F  P  S  T  N  E  I  T  A  P  T  U  O  Y  D
B  D  E  P  A  R  T  M  E  N  T  Y  K  C  I
L  Z  S  D  N  O  I  T  P  E  C  E  R  N  S
G  T  G  Y  I  R  W  R  K  J  G  E  Z  E  P
P  H  A  R  M  A  C  Y  E  F  E  D  T  G  E
K  S  P  M  R  C  T  V  L  C  D  H  T  R  N
U  J  J  D  L  A  Y  R  D  I  O  Q  G  E  S
Q  S  S  I  K  R  M  Y  I  M  J  R  M  M  A
L  T  Q  I  E  D  M  F  A  C  B  L  D  E  R
S  X  U  G  L  I  Q  K  L  D  C  S  H  S  Y
Z  R  R  O  R  O  V  E  Y  H  Z  A  H  G  P
R  U  T  L  K  L  N  X  S  V  L  X  R  J  T
S  S  H  J  Q  O  E  B  I  D  R  B  E  E  C
X  L  T  Y  Q  G  E  R  S  A  K  G  D  A  A
K  P  M  L  Y  Y  G  X  Y  S  E  M  S  O  D
```

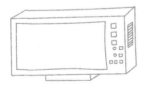

Can you find your way through the maze and back to the nurses station?

Complete this classic sudoku grid by filling in the numbers 1–9 so that each row, each column, and each smaller set of 3 x 3 squares contain each number just once and once only.

			6	4		7		
6	2		1				3	4
	4	7	9					5
7	3	2			9			6
4		5	7	3	6	2		9
		6			2	5		
			8	5		9		7
9		4	2		7			
	7	8	3	9			2	1

DID YOU KNOW

Nurses are said to be referred to as "sisters" because it was once so common for the sick to be cared for during their illness by nuns!

Time for another fiendish test of your logic-solving skills!

Five doctors—Dr. Francis, Dr. Gordon, Dr. Holmes, Dr. Inigo, and Dr. James—have each been assigned to one of five wards in the hospital: Ward 1, Ward 2, Ward 3 Ward 4, and Ward 5. Based on the clues below, can you figure out who has been posted where in the hospital?

1. The person on Ward 5 has a five-letter name.

2. The ward to which Dr. Holmes has been posted is one number lower than the Ward to which Dr. Gordon has been posted...

3. ...and two numbers lower than Dr. Francis' ward!

4. Added together, the numbers of the two wards to which Dr. Gordon and Dr. James have been assigned totals seven.

5. The person with the longest name has been assigned to Ward 3.

DOCTOR	WARD
Dr. Francis	
Dr. Gordon	
Dr. Holmes	
Dr. Inigo	
Dr. James	

Answer the trivia questions at the foot of this page, and fill their answers into the corresponding rows in the grid. Once complete, the name of an item of medical ward equipment will reveal itself down the shaded column.

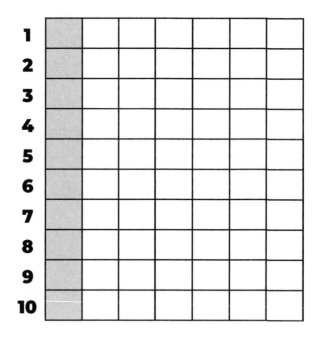

1. What US state is known as Old Dominion?

2. Who was the doomed wife of Orpheus in Greek mythology?

3. In what month of the year do all US elections take place?

4. Bangkok is the capital of what country?

5. What US state is the 6th largest population, but only the 25th largest by area?

6. What Oscar-nominated 2017 movie was the directorial debut of Greta Gerwig? (4,4)

7. What French term is used for a menu on which dishes are listed individually, with separate prices? (1,2,5)

8. What Indian spice is known for its rich yellow color, which has been used in non-culinary contexts as a dye and pigment since antiquity?

9. In dentistry, what condition is defined by a prominent projection of the upper teeth over the lower jaw?

10. What infamous monk and mystic was advisor to the Russian tsar Nicholas II?

How quickly can you solve this quick crossword?

Across

1. Three-dimensional square (4)
3. Most ornate (8)
9. Powerful, extreme (7)
10. Cinema guide (5)
11. Disputing, proving wrong (12)
13. Flee from (6)
15. Chill (6)
17. Clever person (12)
20. Two times (5)
21. Mean amount (7)
22. Came back (8)
23. Untidiness (4)

Down

1. Kids (8)
2. Gnashes (5)
4. Meeting's to-do list (6)
5. Thwarted, undid (12)
6. Improve (7)
7. Ripped (4)
8. Businessman (12)
12. Authenticity (8)
14. Prisoner (7)
16. Make happy (6)
18. Utility (5)
19. Mix with a spoon (4)

Here's a tricky anagram matching game. On the left are the names of eight medical conditions. On the right are the names of the organs and parts of the body they affect—but their names have been jumbled up. Can you unscramble their names, then link them with their matching conditions?

CIRRHOSIS ☐   ☐ 1. NIDYEK

NEPHRITIS ☐   ☐ 2. EARTH

GLAUCOMA ☐   ☐ 3. PINES

ASTHMA ☐   ☐ 4. REVIL

MYOCARDITIS ☐   ☐ 5. LOBOD

LORDOSIS ☐   ☐ 6. YEE

ANEMIA ☐   ☐ 7. CAMSHOT

GASTRITIS ☐   ☐ 8. SLUNG

Each of the 6-letter words below is missing a litter, which fits in the gap.

Once all the words have been filled in, a familiar phrase from the hospital wards will be spelled out down the central column. Watch out, though—there might be multiple possible answers to the missing letters, but only one correct solution overall!

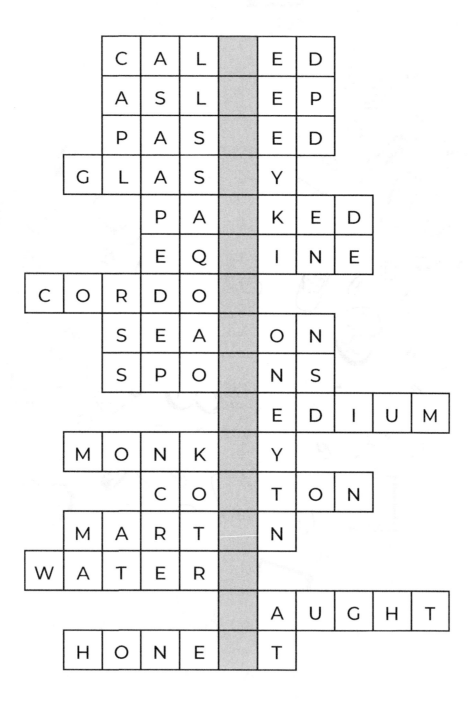

The famous American nurse Jean Watson once said, "Nurses are a unique kind. They have an insatiable need to care for others, which is both ..." what?

To find out the answer, you'll need to crack the code! Answer the trivia questions below, then move each of the answers—letter by letter—into their corresponding numbered boxes in the grid on the opposite page.

1. What American retail brand has a red circle and dot as its logo?

1	2	3	4	5	6

2. A tithe represents one of what fraction of a sum or figure?

7	8	9	10	11

3. What popular sweet treat is made by pouring batter onto a heated iron or pan, marked with a pattern of squares?

12	13	14	15	16	17

4. What type of book takes its name from a character in Greek mythology who was made to support the heavens on his shoulders?

18	19	20	21	22

5. By what five-letter adjective are the largest type of piano known?

23	24	25	26	27

6. In English, what is the third person plural possessive pronoun?

28	29	30	31	32	33

"

7	11	5	31	24

4	32	30	2	19	17	33	10

22	28	3	8	9	23	6	29

21	26	27		14	18	1	13	20

15	16	25	12

•

"

The answers to all the crossword-style clues below can all be made from the letters of the word SURGEON. No letters are used more than once in each answer. Can you work out all ten clues?

SURGEON

1. Compels, pushes forward (4)

   _____

2. Large game bird, similar to a pheasant (6)

   _____

3. Wildebeest (3)

   _____

4. Prickly heathland shrub with yellow flowers (5)

   _____

5. French city, where Joan of Arc was killed (5)

   _____

6. EU single currency (4)

   _____

7. Cosmetic blusher (5)

   _____

8. Snort while snoozing (5)

   _____

9. Ancient writing system of etched straight lines (5)

   _____

10. Spanish title (5)

   _____

All 18 of these internal organs and body parts connect together in the grid below. Can you find out where each one goes?

☐ APPENDIX   ☐ INTESTINE   ☐ STOMACH
☐ ARTERY   ☐ KIDNEYS   ☐ THYROID
☐ BLADDER   ☐ LARYNX   ☐ TONSILS
☐ BONE   ☐ LIVER   ☐ UTERUS
☐ CAPILLARY   ☐ PANCREAS   ☐ VEIN
☐ HEART   ☐ PITUITARY GLAND   ☐ WINDPIPE

The names of 13 people and things you might see in and around a hospital ward are hidden in the grid below. Unlike in an ordinary wordsearch, though, they're not in straight lines! Can you find all the answers, so that no letter is used in multiple words, and all 100 letters are used once with none left over? The first has been filled in for you to make a start.

C	L	O	C	P	A	B	E	D	P
H	E	A	K	I	T	V	I	S	A
N	O	R	N	E	B	P	C	I	N
I	M	T	T	S	O	I	L	T	O
T	R	U	B	E	A	R	S	T	R
O	C	B	S	E	P	D	K	E	S
R	S	R	U	N	E	S	N	A	L
S	E	S	O	R	R	Y	N	E	B
D	O	C	T	S	S	A	I	C	I
L	U	N	C	H	T	R	M	E	D

Hospitals are home to an awful lot of staff, of course! Can you track down all these jobs and roles in the grid below?

- [ ] ANESTHETIST
- [ ] CHAPLAIN
- [ ] CLEANER
- [ ] CONSULTANT
- [ ] DIETICIAN
- [ ] NURSE
- [ ] PHYSICIAN
- [ ] PORTER
- [ ] POSTBOY
- [ ] RECEPTIONIST
- [ ] SURGEON
- [ ] TRIAGE

```
S T C T Z B S W I M P C K F N
W Q D D S U N C W I O L P L T
R R W N R I D D W T S E U J S
D I K G U D T T R X T A I U I
H P E O G R I E W R B N Z V N
G O H P R N S E H J O E L C O
N W E I E H X E T T Y R O S I
P O R T E R I T N I S A O W T
T N A T L U S N O C C E W K P
N T D V T M P E B Y W I N A E
X S U L Q L G M O Q Y W A A C
N I A L P A H C I B S H G N E
P H Y S I C I A N L J G N S R
P T E R U F Z D M L O X Y E M
S B T X K M H E J M B F C D I
```

Here's another quick crossword to get stuck into.

ACROSS

1. Ogle (5)
4. Deceptive schemes (5)
10. Not to be seen or known by other people (7)
11. Rocky slope (5)
12. Ready money (4)
13. Making (8)
15. Comprehends (11)
19. Worries (8)
20. Box, come to blows (4)
23. Grand dramatic musical stage performance (5)
24. Stimulates, invigorates (7)
25. Uses a keyboard (5)
26. Regular order (5)

DOWN

2. Stumbles (5)
3. Makes a noise like a lion (4)
5. Robinson Crusoe, perhaps (8)
6. Wed (7)
7. Room (5)
8. Portrays (11)
9. Roadside (5)
14. Produce (8)
16. Convent (7)
17. Ice cream spoon (5)
18. Traffic collision (5)
21. Middle Eastern flatbread (5)
22. High-ranking playing cards (4)

Complete this classic sudoku grid by filling in the numbers 1–9 so that each row, each column, and each smaller set of 3 x 3 squares contain each number just once and once only.

			1	9				4
					6			
3	1	7			2	9	8	
7					8		3	
						6		
		9		5	4			
	7				9	1		8
4	8		6		1		9	
	9	3	7	8			6	2

DID YOU KNOW

Florence Nightingale, the founder of modern nursing, had a pet owl called Athena.

Can you find your way through the maze and back to the nurses station?

There are five trainee doctors doing the rounds on the wards today: Kate, Leonardo, Micah, Nathan, and Olive. Each of the five eventually wants to specialize in a different field: one wants to become an anesthetist; another wants to go into surgery; someone else wants to be a pediatrician; another wants to try cardiology; and someone else wants to go into orthopedics.

Based only on the clues below, can you figure out who wants to follow what medical specialty?

1. It's one of the boys who wants to go into pediatrics...

2. ...while it's one of the girls who fancies becoming a cardiologist!

3. The trainee anesthetist has a letter N in their name.

4. The person who wants to get into orthopedics has a name that comes alphabetically immediately after that of the girl who wants to become a surgeon.

DOCTOR	FIELD
Kate	
Leonardo	
Micah	
Nathan	
Olive	

Answer the trivia questions at the foot of this page, and fill their answers into the corresponding rows in the grid. Once complete, the name of an item of medical ward equipment will reveal itself down the shaded column.

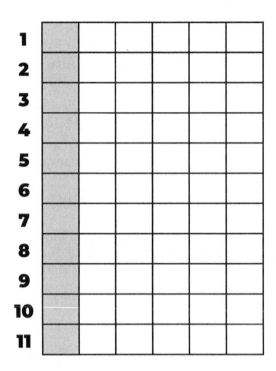

1. What medal is awarded for a second place finish in the Olympic Games?

2. What tropical bird is known for its black and white plumage, and long colorful banana-shaped bill?

3. Which rock band's hits include Hotel California and Take It To The Limit?

4. What is the square root of 144?

5. What is the largest bay in North America?

6. In what English city is the world's oldest university?

7. What kind of educational building takes its name from a Greek word meaning leisure time?

8. Who (surname only) wrote the 1899 novel Heart of Darkness?

9. What US state is the only one to have different designs on opposite sides of its flag?

10. Indigo and violet are shades of what color?

11. On what continent is the Danube river?

Here's another tricky picture puzzle...

How many stethoscopes are tangled together below?

Solve this cryptogram to reveal a nursing one-liner!

"__'M _____ ___' ___ ____L__

"Q'N DPTDQG FZ'TZ ILQEE

W__I_____ ___ __O___

FDQLQWU YW MYVT

__E__ ____U____, ____N,

LZIL TZIVELI, IYW,

S__ ____'__ H____ T__ ___

IY MYV'EE BDXZ LY SZ

__ _____ P_____!"

D EQLLEZ JDLQZWL!"

Here's another quick jumble crossword to unpick. Can you complete the grid below by unscrambling each of the clue words?

1		2			3	■	4	■	
	■		■		5				
6						■		■	
	■		■	■		■		■	
7	8		9			10		11	
■		■		■			■		
			12						
13				■	■			■	
■		■	14						

ACROSS

1. MASTER
5. SATE
6. DISUSE
7. MEDITATES
12. RIOTED
13. MATE
14. SATINS

DOWN

1. MILES
2. STEER
3. AIMED
4. TASTE
8. EVENS
9. MITES
10. TAINT
11. READS

Here's another tricky game of missing letters. Each of the 6-letter words below is missing a letter, which fits in the gap in the shaded column. Once all the words have been completed, a familiar phrase from the hospital wards will be spelled out reading downwards. Watch out, though—there might be multiple possible answers to the missing letters, but only one correct solution overall.

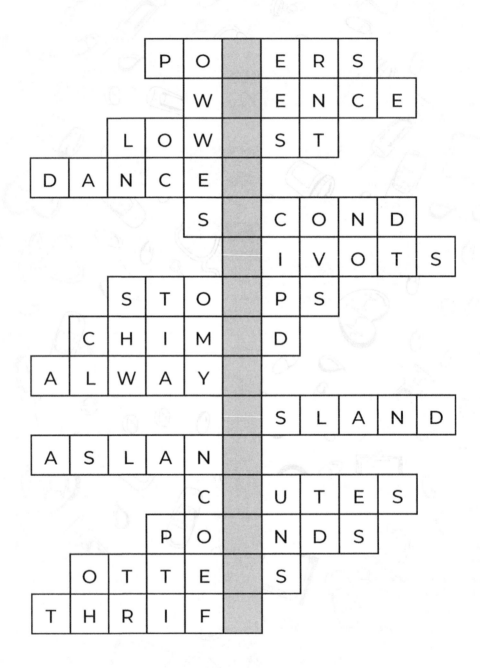

Here's another tricky anagram match. On the left here are the names of eight parts of the human body. On the right are the jumbled names of bones that can be found there. Can you unscramble the answers, then link them with their matching body parts?

CHEST ☐

LEG ☐

KNEE ☐

ARM ☐

BACK ☐

JAW ☐

HEAD ☐

FOOT ☐

☐ 1.RUEMUSH

☐ 2.MICAURN

☐ 3.LEPLATA

☐ 4. MENRUST

☐ 5.SALUT

☐ 6.BALDMINE

☐ 7.TVBEARER

☐ 8. FRUME

The answers to all the crossword-style clues below can all be made from the letters of the word MEDICAL. No letters are used more than once in each answer. Can you work out all ten clues?

MEDICAL

1. Green citrus (4)

_____

2. Maintained, purported (7)

_____

3. Hatred, malevolence (6)

_____

4. Number system based on the digit 10 (7)

_____

5. Put in the post (6)

_____

6. Paper-to-glass transfer (5)

_____

7. Caustic fluid (4)

_____

8. Desert mammal (5)

_____

9. Electronic communication (5)

_____

10. Situated in the middle (6)

_____

Can you find all these treatments, cures, and medications in the grid below?

- ☐ BANDAGE
- ☐ CANNULA
- ☐ DRESSING
- ☐ GAUZE
- ☐ MEDICINE
- ☐ NEEDLE
- ☐ OINTMENT
- ☐ PAINKILLER

- ☐ PILL
- ☐ SLING
- ☐ SPLINT
- ☐ SYRINGE
- ☐ TABLET
- ☐ TOURNIQUET
- ☐ VIAL

```
F  Q  R  U  T  X  J  B  K  P  T  F  R  E  B
G  E  U  P  R  A  L  A  I  V  U  E  S  R  W
C  G  G  N  P  T  B  G  X  W  H  D  D  E  R
A  A  T  K  A  U  E  L  M  Y  E  R  R  L  S
M  D  S  I  E  G  N  E  E  D  L  E  E  L  W
Y  N  V  E  N  A  G  I  S  T  B  C  S  I  J
R  A  R  I  T  N  C  P  T  Y  G  H  S  K  Q
G  B  R  E  I  A  L  U  M  P  B  M  I  N  K
P  Y  R  L  N  I  J  Z  Q  I  G  W  N  I  E
S  U  S  N  N  I  B  P  Q  L  O  A  G  A  S
O  I  U  T  E  I  C  M  Q  L  U  I  U  P  B
V  L  T  O  U  R  N  I  Q  U  E  T  T  Z  J
A  F  Z  B  C  Z  C  A  D  X  L  H  O  H  E
T  N  E  M  T  N  I  O  M  E  H  V  N  K  K
F  G  B  V  I  H  M  A  P  Y  M  M  X  X  L
```

Complete this classic sudoku grid by filling in the numbers 1–9 so that each row, each column, and each smaller set of 3 x 3 squares contain each number just once and once only.

9	4				5	1	7	2	3

9	4			5	1	7	2	3
		6	8	4		1	9	
		1	3	2			4	
2								9
		3	1	9			6	
							7	1
	3			7			1	
	8		2	1	4			7
	6				8		5	4

A first aider is helping out at a local school sports tournament. So far, they've had to treat five of the kids—Brianna, Charles, David, Eduardo, and Freya. Each of the kids has needed something different from the kit: one of them has needed a Band Aid for a cut; another has needed a sling for an injured shoulder; someone has needed ointment for a bee sting; another is complaining of a fever and needed the thermometer; and someone else needed a painkiller for a headache.

Based on the clues below, can you figure out what has been used to treat who?

1. The name of the child who had the headache comes alphabetically between the child who needed the Band Aid and the child who needed the thermometer.

2. One of the three boys wrenched his shoulder while playing in goal during a soccer match, and needed a sling.

3. The person who was stung by a bee has a five-letter name.

4. One of the girls cut her leg while competing in the long jump and needed a Band Aid, while David had to drop out of his long jump competition when he took ill with a fever.

KID	FIRST AID ITEM
Brianna	
Charles	
David	
Eduardo	
Freya	

Can you find your way through the maze and back to the nurses station?

It pretty much takes an army to keep a hospital running every day, of course! The names of 12 hospital workers of all kinds are hidden in the grid below. Unlike in an ordinary wordsearch, though, they're not in straight lines! Can you find all the answers, so that no letter is used in multiple words, and all 100 letters are used once with none left over? The first has been filled in for you to make a start.

C	L	E	A	C	C	O	N	S	U
R	E	T	N	O	O	T	S	P	L
E	P	R	E	R	K	R	U	A	T
F	H	O	E	G	A	I	R	R	A
I	Y	P	N	U	P	E	G	A	N
W	S	E	S	R	H	O	E	M	T
D	I	O	A	P	A	N	D	I	C
I	M	T	R	I	R	M	A	C	I
O	R	H	E	S	T	G	A	R	S
T	C	O	D	R	E	N	E	D	T

Put the answers to these trivia questions into the corresponding rows in the grid. To spell out the name of an item of medical ward equipment down the shaded column.

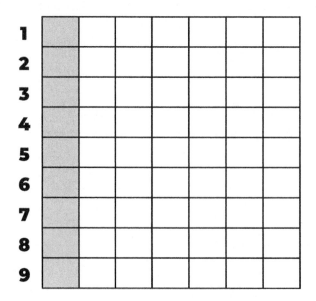

1. What is Africa's most populous country?

2. The subject of a famous play, in Greek mythology who was the daughter of Agamemnon and Clytemnestra?

3. Despite its name, the French fry is believed to have been invented in what European country?

4. In the lyrics to Elvis' hit single Return to Sender, what is wrong with the address on the envelope?

5. What first name connects the US actor Nimoy and the British actor Rossiter?

6. In what European language is the greeting ciao used?

7. What is the North American name for what the Brits would call a post code? (3,4)

8. Which 19th century American essayist and thinker is credited with popularizing the famous maxim that, "Build a better mousetrap, and the world will beat a path to your door"?

9. Which English king was known as The Lionheart?

Here's another tricky game of missing letters. Each of the 6-letter words below is missing a letter, which fits in the gap. Once all the words have been filled in, a familiar phrase from the hospital wards will be spelled out down the central column. Watch out, though—there might be multiple possible answers to the missing letters, but only one correct solution overall!

The completed words (central column letter shown in **bold**):

S _ O U T S	S**H**OUTS
_ U T S E T	**O**UTSET
_ I L L O W	W**W**ILLOW (WILLOW)
P R E _ C H	PRE**A**CH
B U T T E _	BUTTE**R**
E Y _ L I D	EY**E**LID
C E L E R _	CELER**Y**
V I _ L I N	VI**O**LIN
B O _ N D S	BO**U**NDS
C O D I _ Y	CODI**F**Y
P I C K L _	PICKL**E**
N I M B L _	NIMBL**E**
_ O U D E R	**L**OUDER
S A Y _ N G	SAY**I**NG
_ U M B E R	**N**UMBER
T O N _ U E	TON**G**UE

Central column phrase: **HOW ARE YOU FEELING**

The names of these 18 medical fields connect together in the grid below.
Can you find the right homes for all of them?

- ☐ CARDIOLOGY
- ☐ DERMATOLOGY
- ☐ EMERGENCY MEDICINE
- ☐ FORENSICS
- ☐ GERIATRICS
- ☐ IMMUNOLOGY
- ☐ NEUROSURGERY
- ☐ OBSTETRICS
- ☐ ONCOLOGY

- ☐ ORTHOPEDICS
- ☐ PATHOLOGY
- ☐ PEDIATRICS
- ☐ PHARMACOLOGY
- ☐ PHYSIOTHERAPY
- ☐ PSYCHIATRY
- ☐ RADIOLOGY
- ☐ SURGERY
- ☐ UROLOGY

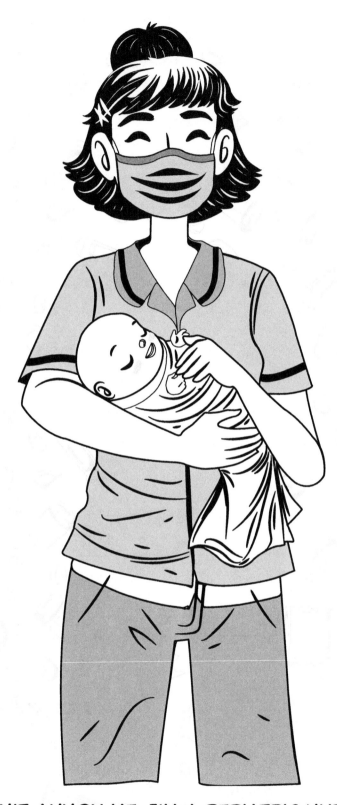

"DON'T ANNOY ME, I'M A PEDIATRIC NURSE—
I HAVE VERY LITTLE PATIENTS..."

On the left here are the names of eight famous actors and actresses. On the right are the jumbled names of the television shows and movies in which they portrayed doctors and nurses. Can you unscramble the answers, then link them with their matching stars?

JULIAN McMAHON ☐   ☐ 1. BRUSSC

DICK VAN DYKE ☐   ☐ 2. GERMANY AS TOY

SANDRA OH ☐   ☐ 3. COTTERGOD HOOD

HUGH LAURIE ☐   ☐ 4. CUTPINK

ZACH BRAFF ☐   ☐ 5. INJURE CAKES

FREDDIE HIGHMORE ☐   ☐ 6. TREELESS HEW

EDIE FALCO ☐   ☐ 7. DISORGANISED RUM

ED FLANDERS ☐   ☐ 8. EOUSH

The answers to all the crossword-style clues below can all be made from the letters of the word INPATIENT. No letters are used any more times than they appear in the original word. Can you work out all ten clues?

INPATIENT

1. In born, natural (6)

_____

2. Renter (6)

_____

3. Discolor, blemish (5)

_____

4. Prong of a fork (4)

_____

5. Legal recognition of invention (6)

_____

6. 1/8th of a gallon (4)

_____

7. Style of bowling (6)

_____

8. Auburn (6)

_____

9. Back of the neck (4)

_____

10. Legendary giant of Greek myth (5)

_____

Can you find all these items of ward equipment and machinery in the grid below?

- AUTOCLAVE
- BLOOD PRESSURE / MONITOR
- DEFIBRILLATOR
- ECG
- FLOWMETER
- INCUBATOR
- IV DRIP

- OXYGEN TANK
- OXYMETER
- SYRINGE PUMP
- ULTRASOUND
- VENTILATOR
- XRAY

```
X O J J Z V Q R C O U E D R A
M D I P M Y E E X L S R E O U
V Q P D F T P Y T Y T U F T T
N G P N E C G R R S R S I A O
Y Y I M L E A I I F U S B L C
I E Y H N S N M E C G E R I L
W X A T O G X T R F F R I T A
O I A U E B F Q L Z L P L N V
V N N P P I R D V I O D L E E
K D U K S O E B Y P W O A V Y
W M E L T V X F P O M O T B E
P D C I S T E V W V E L O H P
I Q N D V J T U U U T B R L Z
U O Q C Q T Y A R X E N S H S
M R O T A B U C N I R X X F H
```

Mother Theresa of Calcutta once famously said that her fellow sisters and carers should, "Let no one come to you without ..." what?

To find out the answer, you'll need to crack this code. Answer the trivia questions below, then move each of the answers—letter by letter—into their corresponding numbered boxes in the grid on the opposite page.

1. What aquatic mammal lives in a dam-like structure known as a lodge?

1	2	3	4	5	6

2. In math, what can be acute, obtuse, right, or reflex?

7	8	9	10	11

3. What boar-like animal with a long snout and black skin and fur is, despite resembling a small elephant, actually most closely related to rhinos?

12	13	14	15	16

4. What is the twenty-first letter of the Greek alphabet, resembling an O with a vertical stroke drawn through it, ϕ?

17	18	19

5. What is the surname of the Batman villain Harvey, better known by his nickname Two Face?

20	21	22	23

"

10	5	13	4	15	8	9

1	21	23	12	11	6

7	22	20

| 18 | 3 | 17 | 14 | 19 | 2 | 16 |
|----|---|----|----|----|---|---| •

"

Complete this classic sudoku grid by filling in the numbers 1–9 so that each row, each column, and each smaller set of 3 x 3 squares contain each number just once and once only.

7	4		3		5		6	8
3		8						
1	6		7	8	4			
		4				2	8	5
8	2			4				
			2	8	6			1
							7	
4	3		8	5			9	6
	9					8	2	4

DID YOU KNOW

On average, a nurse will walk around 3.1 miles (5,000m) in every shift!

Can you find your way through the maze and back to the nurses station?

Six patients in a ward—Mr. Monroe, Mr. Nesbit, Mr. O'Hara, Mr. Peterson, Mr. Quigley, and Mr. Reynolds—have ordered something different from the hospital canteen for their lunch: someone wants chicken soup; another wants a tuna sandwich; someone else wants a cheese roll; another patient has ordered a tomato salad; someone else has ordered a dish of macaroni cheese; and another has ordered a hamburger.

Based on the clues below, can you work out which lunch tray belongs to who?

1. The patient who has ordered the chicken soup has a letter T in their name.

2. Mr. Monroe and Mr. Nesbit are both vegetarian...

3. ...but despite ordering the macaroni cheese, Mr Quigley is not.

4. The surname of the person who ordered the tuna sandwich comes alphabetically immediately after the person who ordered the bean salad, and immediately before the person eating the soup.

PATIENT	LUNCH
Mr. Monroe	
Mr. Nesbit	
Mr. O'Hara	
Mr. Peterson	
Mr. Quigley	
Mr. Reynolds	

Here's another quick jumble crossword to unpick. Can you complete the grid below by unscrambling each of the clue words?

ACROSS

1. HEISTS
5. CHIN
6. GRATIN
7. DREAMIEST
12. CATION
14. RESIST

DOWN

1. TRIED
2. TAXER
3. THIGS
4. CROAT
8. ASIDE
9. NAMES
10. EXITS
11. ARSON

"__ _____T _____S

"SOWHDILWHS HTODBD

_____R _O __ _A_E_,

HBKBO NZ ZH MWSBD,

_____U__ ____H__

RBGWTDB SCBJ CWSB

_I____ ____C___N!"

OYDEYHN OBXBGSYZH!"

Here's another tricky game of missing letters. Each of the 6-letter words below is missing a letter, which fits in the gap. Once all the words have been filled in, a familiar phrase from the hospital wards will be spelled out down the central column. Watch out, though—there might be multiple possible answers to the missing letters, but only one correct solution overall!

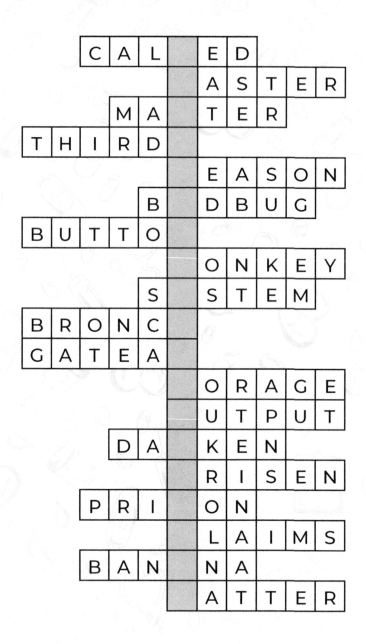

Answer the trivia questions at the foot of this page, and fill their answers into the corresponding rows in the grid. Once complete, the name of an item of medical ward equipment will reveal itself down the shaded column.

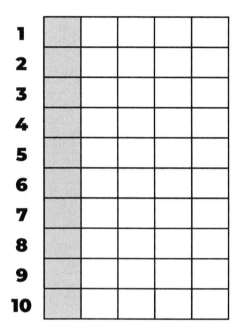

1. What is the largest city in the state of Nebraska?

2. What inert gaseous chemical element, atomic no. 54. takes its name from a Greek word meaning strange or foreign?

3. What family of hardy, aloe-like American plants, with long sword-shaped leaves, includes a white-flowering variety known as the dagger plant?

4. Which former astronaut (surname only) became US senator for Ohio in 1972?

5. The only one of the Seven Wonders of the Ancient World that still stands today is located in what country?

6. What is the only direction it is possible to travel in from the South Pole?

7. The comedian Sacha Baron Cohen appeared as his character Ali G in the music video to what 2000 smash hit by Madonna?

8. Fool's Day is celebrated on the first of what spring month?

9. In the Bible, who is the wife of Abraham and mother of Isaac?

10. Which Czech writer and novelist wrote The Trial and Metamorphosis?

Patients bring all kinds of things with them for a stay in hospital of course! The names of 12 things a patient might bring with them in their overnight bag are hidden in the grid below. Unlike in an ordinary wordsearch, though, they're not in straight lines! Can you find all the answers, so that no letter is used in multiple words, and all 100 letters are used once with none left over? The first has been filled in for you to make a start.

P	H	M	A	G	A	E	A	D	P
P	O	E	N	I	Z	H	N	O	H
U	N	N	O	V	E	L	E	S	C
Z	E	C	H	A	R	W	O	T	H
Z	L	E	B	O	G	E	L	S	A
S	P	H	O	O	E	R	H	S	N
N	G	O	T	K	H	B	S	E	G
A	R	A	P	H	T	R	U	H	E
C	K	S	H	P	O	O	O	T	O
W	A	T	C	E	N	T	L	C	F

WHAT HAPPENED WHEN THE HOSPITAL RAN *OUT OF* MATERNITY NURSES?

THE CONSULTANT HAD A MIDWIFE CRISIS!

Can you find all these parts of a hospital bed in the word search grid below?

- [ ] BEDSHEET
- [ ] BLANKET
- [ ] BRAKE
- [ ] CASTERS
- [ ] CONTROLS
- [ ] CORNERS

- [ ] FOOTBOARD
- [ ] HANDRAIL
- [ ] HEADREST
- [ ] INCLINER
- [ ] MATTRESS
- [ ] PILLOW

```
U  X  H  N  U  C  B  T  W  U  I  U  I  D  S
Z  S  A  U  K  T  S  L  E  R  E  C  O  Z  R
O  K  N  Z  B  E  T  O  A  E  Q  O  U  C  E
F  R  D  R  R  K  Y  O  S  N  H  K  A  P  N
V  E  R  D  P  I  L  L  O  W  K  S  T  M  R
R  H  A  S  D  S  O  G  K  H  T  E  D  F  O
M  E  I  T  S  R  I  E  Z  E  Z  D  T  E  C
H  Z  L  S  T  E  A  O  R  L  L  R  K  Y  B
W  A  P  N  R  E  R  S  F  H  U  A  H  O  N
L  T  O  Q  L  A  T  T  Y  P  K  O  P  P  X
M  C  X  N  G  L  Y  Z  T  C  W  B  W  R  P
I  N  C  L  I  N  E  R  T  A  P  T  Z  L  G
H  V  V  W  J  H  B  K  E  T  M  O  R  K  I
G  F  X  S  Z  J  L  X  C  M  W  O  D  O  Z
E  K  A  R  B  Y  V  X  C  J  T  F  H  L  O
```

Here's another tricky anagram match. On the left here are the names of eight descriptions of body parts. On the right are the jumbled names of the body parts to which they relate. Can you unscramble the answers, then link them correctly?

Largest blood vessel ☐   ☐ 1.FRUME

Longest legbone ☐   ☐ 2.PASTES

Smallest bone ☐   ☐ 3.YESLIED

Longest nerve ☐   ☐ 4. ACRONE

Thinnest skin ☐   ☐ 5.TORAA

Heaviest internal organ ☐   ☐ 6.TUESLUG

Largest muscle ☐   ☐ 7.VILER

Only body part without a blood supply ☐   ☐ 8.ISCACTI

The radiography department has quite a queue of appointments today! Six patients—Mrs. Robinson, Mrs. Sanchez, Mr. Thomas, Mr. Underwood, Mr. Vincent, and Miss Williams—are currently sat in the waiting room, each one needing an x-ray on a different part of their body: one person has bumped their head and needs an x-ray of their skull; another has broken their wrist; someone else has bruised a rib; another person needs an extra of their recent hip surgery; someone else has hurt their leg and needs to tell if it's broken; and another person has tripped and broken their toe.

Based on the clues below, can you work out who needs what bone x-raying?

1. The person who had hip surgery is a woman.

2. Mr. Underwood has not bruised his ribs.

3. The lady who tripped and has apparently broken her toe has an A in her name.

4. The name of the man who bumped his head comes alphabetically immediately before the lady who has slipped and broken her wrist.

PATIENT	BONE
Mrs. Robinson	
Mrs. Sanchez	
Mr. Thomas	
Mr. Underwood	
Mr. Vincent	
Miss Williams	

Complete this classic sudoku grid by filling in the numbers 1–9 so that each row, each column, and each smaller set of 3 x 3 squares contain each number just once and once only.

5	1		3				2	
6	8		7		9	3		5
	7		5		6		8	
1		6			4	8	7	
	9	8		7	3			4
				8	2		9	3
		1		6				
9	6	7	2	3			1	
	5			9				

Can you find your way through the maze and back to the nurses station?

The answers to all the crossword-style clues below can all be made from the letters of the word PHYSICIAN. No letters are used any more times than they appear in the original word. Can you work out all ten clues?

PHYSICIAN

1. Iron-rich leaf vegetable (7)

   _____

2. Country where Barcelona is located (5)

   _____

3. Metal fastener made of interlocking hoops (5)

   _____

4. Porcelain (5)

   _____

5. Responds anxiously or terrifiedly (6)

   _____

6. Soreness (4)

   _____

7. Pointy, prickly (5)

   _____

8. Ancient Indian board game (7)

   _____

9. Coordinate audio and video (4)

   _____

10. Having a flavor like CLUE 1! (8)

   _____

President Barack Obama once famously described nurses as … what?

To find out the answer, you'll need to crack this code. Answer the trivia questions below, then move each of the answers—letter by letter—into their corresponding numbered boxes in the grid on the opposite page.

1. What South American country is named for the fact that the equator passes directly through it?

1	2	3	4	5	6	7

2. What was the name of Microsoft's email service, which was relaunched as Outlook in 2012?

8	9	10	11	12	13	14

3. A sleuth is the collective noun for which large carnivorous mammals?

15	16	17	18	19

4. What aromatic Mediterranean herb, often paired with rosemary, is actually a close relative of oregano?

20	21	22	23	24

5. What 2020 science fiction movie, directed by Christopher Nolan, told the story of a CIA agent who manipulates the flow of time to save the world?

25	26	27	28	29

6. What small sweet-tasting purplish fruits, often served warm or roasted, are the edible fruits of the Ficus tree?

30	31	32	33

"

10	21	24

15	28	4	20	31	27	32

8	26	12	18	25

6	20

9	3	7

23	1	5	13	2	17	14

19	22	33	29	16	11

●

"

Here's a tricky play on a classic sudoku game. Can you complete the grid so that each item—the clock, the bed, the pen, the clipboard, the thermometer, and the telephone—appear just once in each row, column, and box of six squares?

☎	🌡	🛏		🖊	
			☎	🛏	
		🌡	🖊	🕐	📋
	📋	🕐			☎
					🖊

The names of two items basic items of medical equipment—both seven letters long—have been jumbled together here. Can you pull them apart?

AABDEEGGINNRSY

Here's one for the phlebotomist on the ward! All the words below are either types or names of blood vessels in the human body. Can you find the correct places for them all in the grid so that they all connect together?

- [ ] AORTA
- [ ] ARTERIOLE
- [ ] AURICULAR
- [ ] AXILLARY
- [ ] BRACHIAL
- [ ] CAROTID
- [ ] CELIAC
- [ ] CERVICAL
- [ ] EPIGASTRIC
- [ ] FEMORAL
- [ ] GASTRIC
- [ ] ILIAC
- [ ] POPLITEAL
- [ ] RADIAL
- [ ] RENAL
- [ ] SACRAL
- [ ] STYLOMASTOID
- [ ] SUBCLAVIAN
- [ ] ULNAR
- [ ] VEIN
- [ ] VENA CAVA
- [ ] VENA COMITANS
- [ ] VIDIAN

Time for another missing letters game. Each of these 6-letter words is missing a letter. Once all these letters have been filled in, a phrase from the hospital wards will be spelled out down the central column. Watch out, though—there might be multiple possible answers to the missing letters, but only one correct solution overall!

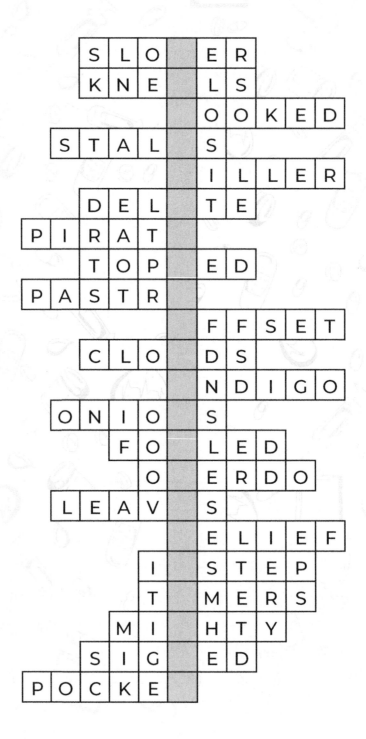

Answer the trivia questions at the foot of this page, and fill their answers into the corresponding rows in the grid. Once complete, the name of an item of medical ward equipment will reveal itself down the shaded column.

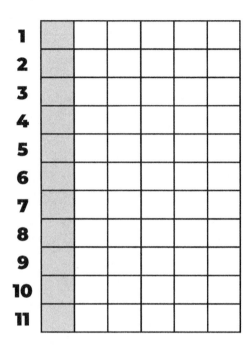

1. In what solo racket sport is a score of zero known as "love"?

2. What name links Catherine, a wife of Henry VIII, Ron, a famous Hollywood moviemaker, and Trevor, a classic British actor who died in 1987?

3. What is the fifth prime number?

4. Which formers US president (surname only) died in 2004?

5. What is the capital city of Spain?

6. The French liqueur Triple sec is flavored with what fruit?

7. Chihuahua dogs are named after a state in which Latin American country?

8. What is the name of the equatorial Pacific Ocean current whose annual appearance and movement can affect the entire climate of the globe? (2,4)

9. Which of Jesus' disciples was known as the "Doubting"?

10. What was the name of the English king whose marriage to Wallis Simpson triggered an abdication crisis?

11. What name is given to the large steering board at the back of a ship?

Complete this classic sudoku grid by filling in the numbers 1–9 so that each row, each column, and each smaller set of 3 x 3 squares contain each number just once and once only.

6	7	1	4	3		8	5	2
4	2				8			3
		9					7	1
3	4				2	5		7
		8	3	6		2		
		7					8	
	6		9		3	1	2	
	1		5	8				
7			2	4	1		9	

DID YOU KNOW

January 27th is officially
School Nurse Day
worldwide!

It's a quiet night on the hospital ward, and there are six overnight nursing staff—Anne, Brian, Catherine, David, Ellie, and Freda—currently monitoring patients in six wardrooms: Room 1, Room 2, Room 3, Room 4, Room 5, and Room 6.

At the moment, there is one nurse in each room.

Based on the clues below, can you work out which nurse is in which room?

1. The name of the nurse in Room 1 does not end in a vowel.

2. The nurse who is currently doing the rounds in Room 5 has a five-letter name.

3. Anne is currently in the room one number lower than David, and two numbers lower than the room Catherine is currently in.

4. Freda is in a room next door to Brian on one side, and Ellie on the other.

ROOM no.	nurse
1	
2	
3	
4	
5	
6	

Nurses have to keep track of an awful lot of patients' facts and figures. How many of them can you find in the grid below?

- ☐ BLOOD PRESSURE
- ☐ BLOOD TYPE
- ☐ BODY MASS INDEX
- ☐ BONE DENSITY
- ☐ BREATHING RATE
- ☐ CONSCIOUSNESS
- ☐ HEART RATE

- ☐ HEIGHT
- ☐ METABOLIC RATE
- ☐ OXYGEN / SATURATION
- ☐ REFLEXES
- ☐ TEMPERATURE
- ☐ WEIGHT

```
E  I  N  V  Y  H  Q  Q  S  Y  S  R  B  O  O
R  D  J  E  R  B  E  E  A  A  K  L  D  X  Y
U  Q  A  F  B  C  X  A  T  E  O  V  X  Y  X
T  B  S  E  J  E  V  U  R  O  E  M  S  G  I
A  H  U  P  L  V  R  A  D  T  E  G  P  E  Y
R  Z  E  F  W  A  X  P  W  M  R  E  O  N  T
E  C  E  I  T  I  R  N  E  K  Y  A  O  Q  I
P  R  G  I  G  E  M  G  I  U  Z  J  T  U  S
M  S  O  L  S  H  P  H  G  C  P  Y  Y  E  N
E  N  Z  S  A  W  T  W  H  B  G  P  Y  B  E
T  E  U  E  I  E  P  Y  T  D  O  O  L  B  D
W  R  M  E  T  A  B  O  L  I  C  R  A  T  E
E  E  T  A  R  G  N  I  H  T  A  E  R  B  N
S  S  E  N  S  U  O  I  C  S  N  O  C  L  O
B  O  D  Y  M  A  S  S  I  N  D  E  X  R  B
```

Can you find your way through the maze and back to the nurses station?

Time for another break! How quickly can you solve this quick crossword?

ACROSS

7. Someone called the same (8)
8. Sharp tasting (4)
9. Cook meat (4)
10. Preceding (8)
11. Ahead (7)
13. Twig (5)
16. Series, regular sequence (5)
17. Joking, making gags (7)
19. Newsflash (8)
21, Soreness
22. Bovine meat (4)
23. University lessons (8)

DOWN

1. Sort, type (8)
2. Phobia (4)
3. Blood-sucker (7)
4. Separate, amputate (5)
5. Helped (8)
6. Ballerina's skirt (4)
12. Fauna (8)
14. Think about, mull (8)
15. Outdoor meals (7)
18. Fashion (5)
20. Employs (4)
21. Add (4)

Your anatomical knowhow should be pretty good, of course... but this is a tricky test of just how much you know! The names of 16 human bones are hidden in the grid below. Unlike in an ordinary wordsearch, though, they're not in straight lines! Can you find all the answers, so that no letter is used in multiple words, and all 100 letters are used once with none left over? The first has been filled in for you to make a start.

P	A	R	E	L	B	M	A	L	A
E	T	U	S	C	I	D	N	C	V
L	E	M	S	A	P	U	L	A	I
L	R	P	T	Y	O	I	D	S	C
A	L	E	E	H	L	L	U	K	L
F	V	I	R	N	U	M	C	O	E
I	B	S	M	E	R	U	S	C	C
L	U	H	U	U	I	D	A	R	Y
A	B	I	C	S	A	N	E	R	X
T	I	A	A	L	C	S	U	I	B

The answers to all the crossword-style clues below can all be made from the letters of the word AMBULANCE. No letters are used any more times than they appear in the original word. Can you work out all ten clues?

AMBULANCE

1. Not capable of doing (6)

_____

2. Bone of the forearm (4)

_____

3. Hygienic, sterilized (5)

_____

4. Trite, boring (5)

_____

5. Explanatory guidebook (6)

_____

6. Set of scales (7)

_____

7. Wrist restraint (7)

_____

8. Make still or tranquil (6)

_____

9. Egg white (7)

_____

10. Untie a shoe, say (6)

_____

"IS THIS YOUR FIRST CHILD?"
"NO, THIS IS MY HUSBAND."

"__ _N_ L_____ D__

"FJ JFN AYLQNFNH QJ

____ _O____'_ A_____

QPN HJCQJG'L VHSYCN

_____ T_I__ __ _____S___E.

VEJRQ RLYFZ VF JQJLCJMN.

__ ___T __ ___ E__ ___ _U_

YQ BNFQ YF JFN NVG VFH JRQ

___ __H__."

QPN JQPNG."

Here's another quick jumble crossword to unpick. Can you complete the grid below by unscrambling each of the clue words?

1		2		3		4		5
6								
				7				
8								
9			10				11	
12								
				13				
14								

ACROSS

4. DAM

6. RENAL

7. MALIC

8. ROUGE

10. RUNES

12. VOTER

13. PAEAN

14. ROPES

DOWN

1. URLS

2. NOSEGUARD

3. CONE

4. GERANIUMS

5. MADE

9. OPTS

10. EARN

11. LANE

Here's another tricky game of missing letters. Each of the 6-letter words below is missing a letter, which fits in the gap. Once all the words have been filled in, a familiar phrase from the hospital wards will be spelled out down the central column. Watch out, though—there might be multiple possible answers to the missing letters, but only one correct solution overall!

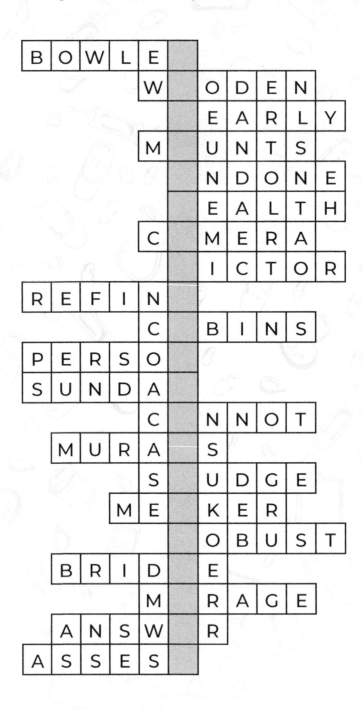

There are seven consultants on the ward: Dr. Andrews, Dr. Blair, Dr. Chavez, Dr. Dorfman, Dr. Ellis, Dr. Farouk, and Dr. Graham. Each one does their rounds on a different day of the week.

Based on the clues below, can you figure out who is assigned to which day?

1. Dr. Graham works the day before Dr. Farouk, who in turn does his rounds the day before Dr. Blair does hers.

2. Neither Dr. Andrews nor Dr. Ellis work on Fridays.

3. The doctor who does their rounds on a Wednesday has a letter R in their name...

4. ...while the two doctors who do their rounds on the weekend have an H in their names.

5. Dr. Farouk does his rounds on a day with a six-letter name.

CONSULTANT	DAY
Dr. Andrews	
Dr. Blair	
Dr. Chavez	
Dr. Dorfman	
Dr. Ellis	
Dr. Farouk	
Dr. Graham	

Answer the trivia questions at the foot of this page, and fill their answers into the corresponding rows in the grid. Once complete, the name of an item of medical equipment will reveal itself down the shaded column.

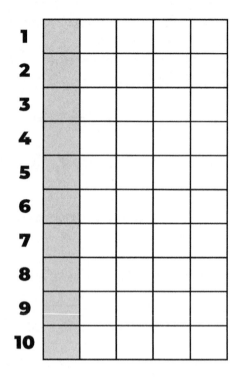

1. Which great Asian nation was once ruled by the Qi dynasty?

2. Which British classical composer (surname only) wrote the famous Enigma Variations?

3. Who is Bill Sykes' girlfriend in Charles Dickens' novel Oliver Twist?

4. What is the largest of the lower 48 states?

5. What name is given to the front-facing upright portion of a step?

6. In what country was Priyanka Chopra born?

7. What soft sweet confectionary is made from heating and mixing sugar, butter, and milk?

8. According to some interpretations of the New Testament, how was Joseph of Arimathea related to Jesus, or else to his mother Mary?

9. The phrase hoi polloi is taken from what ancient language?

10. Which celebrity talkshow ran for more than 3,000 episodes across 19 seasons, until its final episode on May 26, 2022?

Complete this classic sudoku grid by filling in the numbers 1–9 so that each row, each column, and each smaller set of 3 x 3 squares contain each number just once and once only.

6		5	4			7		9
	7			5		1	6	4
	4	3		7	9			
				6	8	9		
	2					6	7	
7			3			4	5	1
			9	1			4	2
	9	4			6	5		7
2						3		6

The great Maya Angelou once famously said that although a patient may forget a nurse's name, they will never ... what?

To find out the answer, you'll need to crack this code. Answer the trivia questions below, then move each of the answers—letter by letter—into their corresponding numbered boxes in the grid on the opposite page.

1. In what sport might you score an albatross?

1	2	3	4

2. What is the name of the character voiced by Tom Hanks in the Toy Story movies?

5	6	7	8	9

3. The Oscar-winning title song to what 1980 musical was performed by Irene Cara?

10	11	12	13

4. What is the world's second-tallest bird after the ostrich?

14	15	16

5. What a cuspids, bicuspids, and canines?

17	18	19	20	21

6. By what three-letter name is US R&B superstar Gabriella Sarmiento Wilson known?

22	23	24

"

4	6	24	1	23	20

21	7	5

9	2	16

12	11	8	18

17	22	14	15

| 10 | 13 | 19 | 3 |
|----|----|----|---| •

"

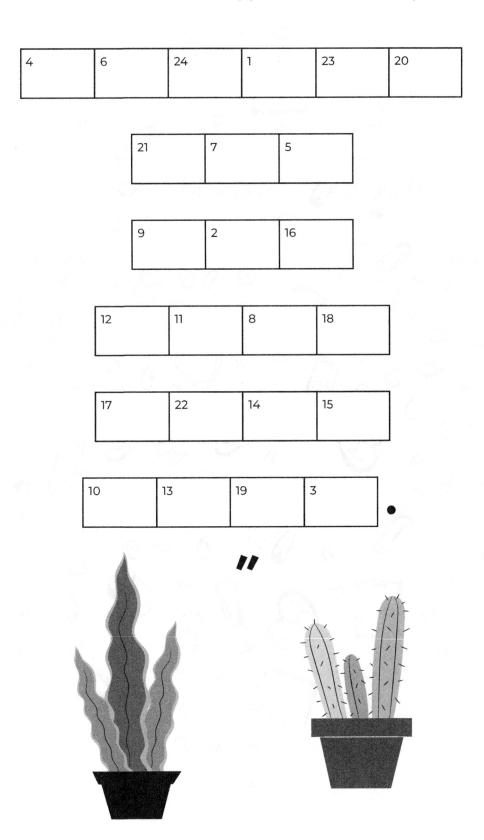

How's your bedside manner?

☐ ANY ACHES / AND PAINS?
☐ ANY BETTER / TODAY?
☐ ARE YOU / COMFORTABLE?
☐ CAN I GET YOU / ANYTHING?
☐ DO YOU HAVE / A TEMPERATURE?
☐ DO YOU NEED / ME TO CALL / ANYBODY?
☐ HOW ARE YOU?
☐ HOW DID / YOU SLEEP?
☐ THIS MIGHT / STING A LITTLE!
☐ WHERE DOES / IT HURT

```
S  C  Q  Z  H  M  D  Y  S  H  G  C  F  T  E
X  E  X  A  R  U  O  T  N  O  B  A  N  H  O
R  G  O  H  Q  U  Y  R  I  W  L  N  C  G  J
H  Y  M  D  S  D  O  U  A  A  L  I  O  I  G
D  F  X  L  E  C  U  H  P  R  A  G  H  M  N
E  T  E  S  K  R  N  T  D  E  C  E  O  S  I
V  E  V  O  W  A  E  I  N  Y  O  T  W  I  H
P  R  B  O  R  M  E  H  A  O  T  Y  D  H  T
A  R  E  Y  O  U  D  K  W  U  E  O  I  T  Y
A  N  Y  B  E  T  T  E  R  O  M  U  D  F  N
D  O  Y  O  U  H  A  V  E  F  D  J  C  A  A
U  E  L  B  A  T  R  O  F  M  O  C  T  Y  Y
A  N  Y  B  O  D  Y  S  E  H  C  A  Y  N  A
G  T  I  E  R  U  T  A  R  E  P  M  E  T  A
S  T  I  N  G  A  L  I  T  T  L  E  W  E  R
```

Can you find your way through the maze and back to the nurses station?

Can you unjumble tomorrow's lunch menu?

Today's Menu

☑ STARTER

CHASED LEASE

☑ MAINS

HAREM GRUB

EAGLET WEB VEST

☑ DESSERT

ECLECTIC AROMA ECHO

The names of two common symptoms—one an 8-letter word, the other a 9-letter word—are jumbled up here. Can you unscramble them?

AACDDEEEHHIINSSZZ

Here's another quick crossword to get stuck into.

ACROSS

1. Aroma (5)
4. Waterway (5)
10. Deceitful, scheming (7)
11. Sag (5)
12. Apply pressure (4)
13. Interrogative (8)
15. See-through (11)
19. Financial (8)
20. Angel's headband (4)
23. Water vapor (5)
24. Organic (7)
25. Lamps (anag., 5)
26. Calls like a donkey (5)

DOWN

2. Caverns (5)
3. Midday (4)
5. Manufacture (8)
6. Feeling (7)
7. Adjust (5)
8. Expectations, presumed truths (11)
9. Backbone (5)
14. Relaxed (8)
16. Unlocks again (7)
17. Untidy (5)
18. Chills (5)
21. Range (5)
22. Asterisk, pointed shape (4)

Here's another tricky game of missing letters. Each of the 6-letter words below is missing a letter, which fits in the gap. Once all the words have been filled in, a familiar phrase from the hospital wards will be spelled out down the central column. Watch out, though—there might be multiple possible answers to the missing letters, but only one correct solution overall!

```
M U S C L [ ]
      B O [ ] K E D
         [ ] N K I N D
         [ ] H E A T S
         [ ] L W A Y S
C O U P O [ ]
P I N I N [ ]
         [ ] U D E R    (L [ ] U D E R)
E N O U G [ ]
         [ ] U N D S    (S [ ] U N D S)
         [ ] O T I O N
    C R E [ ] P S
      L I [ ] T L E
         [ ] M E D Y    (C [ ] M E D Y)
         [ ] E C E N T
C E L L [ ] R
         [ ] O N D E R
```

Here's one last anagram match to get stuck into—and once more, we're putting your medical and anatomical knowledge to the test! On the left here are the names of eight parts of the body. On the right are the names of the larger organs and body parts those on the left are considered part of—only their names have been jumbled up! Can you unscramble the answers, then link them with their matching components?

ISLETS OF LANGERHANS	☐	☐	1. NIRAB
ALVEOLI	☐	☐	2. SATCHMO
EPIDERMIS	☐	☐	3. CRANAPES
AMYGDALA	☐	☐	4. ELVIS P
GASTRIC FUNDUS	☐	☐	5. EARTH
ACETABULUM	☐	☐	6. NOUGET
PULMONARY VALVE	☐	☐	7. SINK
LINGUAL PAPILLAE	☐	☐	8. SLUNG

The answers to all the crossword-style clues below can all be made from the letters of the word TREATMENT. No letters are used any more times than they appear in the original word. Can you work out all ten clues?

TREATMENT

1. Nastier, more unpleasant (6)

_____

2. Far East noodle dish (5)

_____

3. Make an animal less wild (4)

_____

4. Be important (6)

_____

5. Ferret-like animal (6)

_____

6. Not glossy, having a lightly slightly dulled finish (5)

_____

7. 100cm (5)

_____

8. Give a new title to (6)

_____

9. Chat casually (6)

_____

10. Plead, beseech (7)

_____

"I'D SAY YOU'RE TOO BADLY INJURED TO DISCHARGE YOURSELF, SIR, BUT HEY—SUTURE SELF!"

There's a lot more to a hospital that just wards and clinics, of course! The names of 12 other buildings and facilities you'll find in and around a hospital are hidden in the grid below. Unlike in an ordinary wordsearch, though, they're not in straight lines! Can you find all the answers, so that no letter is used in multiple words, and all 100 letters are used once with none left over? The first has been filled in for you to make a start.

P	A	R	K	R	E	S	T	A	U
C	G	N	I	R	E	S	S	E	R
H	L	O	T	D	S	H	O	R	A
A	H	A	I	R	O	C	W	E	N
P	G	A	R	D	N	V	S	R	T
E	L	G	Y	E	N	E	E	C	A
C	E	P	M	N	S	N	R	E	F
O	C	T	I	O	T	I	O	T	S
F	E	R	H	O	O	E	N	C	E
F	E	E	S	P	I	L	E	T	S

We're almost at the end! Time to put your feet up in the break room with this crisscross grid. Can you find the right home for all these break room essentials?

- ☐ ARMCHAIR
- ☐ BOOKCASE
- ☐ CAKE
- ☐ CHEESE
- ☐ COFFEE MACHINE
- ☐ CREAMER
- ☐ CUSHION
- ☐ FOOTSTOOL
- ☐ FRESH AIR
- ☐ FRIENDS
- ☐ GOSSIPS
- ☐ MAGAZINES
- ☐ MILK
- ☐ MUSIC
- ☐ NAP
- ☐ NEWSPAPERS
- ☐ PUZZLE BOOK
- ☐ RADIO
- ☐ READ
- ☐ REST
- ☐ SANDWICHES
- ☐ SNACKS
- ☐ SNOOZE
- ☐ SODA
- ☐ TEA
- ☐ TEAPOT
- ☐ TELEVISION
- ☐ VENDING MACHINE
- ☐ WATER COOLER
- ☐ WINDOW

Complete this classic sudoku grid by filling in the numbers 1–9 so that each row, each column, and each smaller set of 3 x 3 squares contain each number just once and once only.

	6	9	4	1	2	3	7	
		1						8
	7		8	9				
	9	6	1	8	3	5	4	7
	3					6	8	
4	8	5				9	3	
		8				7		
			7	6	8	1	2	
	2		9		1	8	6	4

Can you find your way through the maze and back to the nurses station?

Here's one final jumble crossword to solve. Can you complete the grid below by unscrambling each of the clue words?

ACROSS

3. NOD
5. MAPLE
7. IDOLS
8. THORN
10. DINGY
12. DARED
13. AUGER
14. TOADY

DOWN

1. WAND
2. HEMS
3. INDULGED
4. DONE
6. DEPRAVED
9. TARN
10. YARD
11. EGOS

Solve this cryptogram to reveal a nursing one-liner!

" _ _ S, _ _ O _ _ _ _ _ _ _ A _

"PGV, E NIBLY XCOX

P _ _ _ E _ _ T _ _ _ _ _ H _ _ L _ _ _ .

ZOXEGLX XCOX E COY

_ _ _ _ _ N _ C _ _ _ _ _ , _ _ W _ _ _ N _ . _ . _ ."

MIVX. EFILETOMMP, CG DOV EL E.T.B."

Time for discharge! One last wordsearch covering a patient's last day on the ward.

- [ ] CAR KEYS
- [ ] CHILDREN
- [ ] CHOCOLATES
- [ ] CLEAN SHEETS
- [ ] FAMILY
- [ ] FLOWERS
- [ ] FRIENDS
- [ ] GOODBYE
- [ ] HANDSHAKES
- [ ] HAT AND COAT
- [ ] HUGS
- [ ] LAUNDRY
- [ ] PACKED BAGS
- [ ] THANK YOUS
- [ ] TRANSPORT

```
O S T D J R H G G Y L G H T N
M E Q C W E A O C F L U W E W
M I O L T E N O J A G I R D K
I D G K R Z D D G S R D M C I
F L O W E R S B W Q L K H A H
T T S W Z J H Y Y I K O E N F
H H G S A O A E H K C Q I Y F
I T A N D N K C G O B E Z N S
C S B N I C E Y L Y T K A V E
M D D O K W S A T Z S H Z B E
Y N E B Q Y T R O P S N A R T
T E K P Y E O Z L V M G S U Y
R I C T S L A U N D R Y U J D
Z R A C L E A N S H E E T S M
R F P T T A O C D N A T A H I
```

Inside one of the cabinets on the ward there are eight shelves. The cabinet contains all sorts of equipment, of course, but alongside everything else, there are bandages on one shelf; on another there are syringes; another is where the sterile gloves are kept; there is a pair of scissors on one; another has a box of cotton swabs; hand sanitizer is on one shelf; there is an otoscope on another; and finally, a thermometer. Based on the clues below, can you figure out which item—bandages, syringes, gloves, scissors, swabs, sanitizer, otoscope, thermometer—is on which shelf?

1. The thermometer is on the shelf below the sanitizer, and the gloves are kept above the syringes.

2. The bandages—which are not on Shelf 4—are on the shelf above the scissors.

3. The items on Shelf 5 and Shelf 7 both begin and end with an S...

4. ...while the item on Shelf 2 ends in an R.

5. The item with the shortest name is on the shelf immediately below the item with the longest name.

SHELF	ITEM
1 (Top)	
2	
3	
4	
5	
6	
7	
8 (Bottom)	

110

Answer the trivia questions at the foot of this page, and fill their answers into the corresponding rows in the grid. Once complete, the name of an item of medical ward equipment will reveal itself down the shaded column.

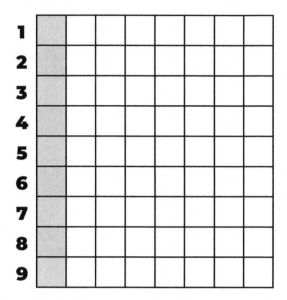

1. What Australian city is the state capital of South Australia?

2. What comes after antepenultimate and penultimate?

3. In Greek mythology, who was the son of the god of night, Nyx, who was seen as the personification of death?

4. Which is America's Sooner State?

5. What nationality are the pop artists Shania Twain, Bryan Adams, and Celine Dion?

6. How is the Cavalier described in the title of a famous 1624 portrait by Frans Hals?

7. Who won an Oscar for his role in Scent of a Woman? (2,6)

8. Who was queen of England from 1837 to 1901?

9. Which famous physicist (surname only) was awarded the 1921 Nobel Prize in Physics?

Here's last quick crossword to round things off!

Across

1. Quickly submerges and removes from liquid (4)
3. Three dots used to show omission (8)
9. Options (7)
10. Assessed the duration of (5)
11. Overlook, fail to see (4,3,5)
13. Main course (6)
15. Prey, predator's target (6)
17. Mixtures (12)
20. Newspapers, for instance (5)
21. Sentimental singer (7)
22. Compassion (8)
23. Writing implements (4)

Down

1. Winter month (8)
2. Puddles (5)
4. Diminish (6)
5. Preface (12)
6. Marines (anag., 7)
7. Fizzy drink (4)
8. Muddle-headed person (12)
12. Ugly sights (8)
14. Stood upon (7)
16. Raps upon a door (6)
18. 1/16th of a pound (5)
19. Run _____, to go berserk (4)

"DON'T WIND ME UP – REMEMBER,
I STICK NEEDLES IN PEOPLE FOR A LIVING."

CONCLUSION

And with that last puzzle (and one last gag!) we're finished! Your Ultimate Nurse Activity Book for Nurses is complete.

We really hope you enjoyed the fun games and activities that have kept you busy for the past 100 pages or so! And who knows, as well as keeping your brain ticking over and gray matter engaged, perhaps you've picked up a little something you never know along the way? Or perhaps, for that matter, you've just learned a new one-liner to try down on the wards next time you're in...?

But now, it's time for a well-earned rest before that next shift begins. Time for a quick cup of tea? Sounds like a great idea to me!

SOLUTIONS

6

```
U S F G C P E F I V V O E D U
D E R U T C A R F U C A N O T
E N O B N E K O R B B U N F R
D O K H H X I B I N O M R R I
S I J C K B P B A W T A Q F P
L T A A S G P P E C N L E W S
G A O M Q N O R E I N V X R A
K R O O J J U U M S E A Q X N
H E C T X T Q A N R I J O H D
J C B S C Z L R U I C U T S F
B A I N C B U N X M E P R G A
E L U I I B S P R A I N D B L
S P X T I A J A Y R V B A V L
C A E A F O Y J R X Z F D D S
X I B H H P N Z A Y G H S F R
```

8

1	6	9	4	5	7	2	3	8
4	2	3	9	6	8	5	7	1
5	7	8	1	3	2	6	4	9
2	8	5	7	1	9	3	6	4
6	1	4	5	2	3	9	8	7
9	3	7	6	8	4	1	2	5
3	9	6	8	7	5	4	1	2
8	5	2	3	4	1	7	9	6
7	4	1	2	9	6	8	5	3

7

CALAMINE
SCISSORS
COTTONWOOL
ANTISEPTICWIPE
SAFETYPIN
GAUZE
EMERGENCYBLANKET
TWEEZERS
TAPE
LOTION
HANDSANITIZER
BANDAGES

9

10

PATIENT	INJURY
Mrs. Adams	Knee
Mr. Bryant	Finger
Mrs. Charles	Head
Mr. Davison	Shoulder
Mrs. Edmunds	Hand

Heart, Tongue, Spleen, Kidney, Tonsil, Gall Bladder, Diaphragm.

14

WATCH and THERMOMETER.

11

There are 27 clipboards.

15

TOMATO SOUP

CHICKEN PIE

MACARONI CHEESE

FRUIT SALAD

12

1.Polish, 2. Pilot, 3. Postal, 4. Pathos, 5. Spoilt, 6. Hilt, 7. Patio, 8. Pistol, 9. Hoist, 10. Alto

16

S	P	A	R	S	E	
A		T				A
T	A	L	K	S		S
I		A		P		L
N		S	H	O	R	E
S			R			E
	I	N	S	T	E	P

13

S	T	O	M	A	N	I	X	L	L
P	A	A	R	C	T	E	N	A	U
C	N	I	B	H	T	S	Y	R	N
R	S	N	T	H	I	T	R	A	G
E	K	I	N	Y	N	G	H	E	S
A	T	O	N	R	E	A	L	L	B
S	E	U	G	O	I	D	M	G	L
E	N	K	Y	T	I	A	P	A	A
E	L	I	E	O	D	E	H	R	D
S	P	D	N	N	G	U	R	E	D

ANSWERS: Stomach, Intestine, Larynx, Lungs, Pancreas, Brain, Skin, Thyroid,

17

"My x-ray appointment at the hospital took ages today, because they only had a skeleton staff!"

18

```
F P S T N E I T A P T U O Y D
B D E P A R T M E N T Y K C I
L Z S D N O I T P E C E R N S
G T G Y I R W R K J G E Z E P
P H A R M A C Y E F E D T R E
K S P M R C T V L C D H T N G
U J J D L A Y R D I O Q G E S
Q S S I K R M Y I M J R M M A
L T Q I E D M F A C B L D E R
S X U G L I Q K L D C S H S Y
Z R R O R O V E Y H Z A H G P
R U T L K L N X S V L X R J T
S S H J Q O E B I D R B E E C
X L T Y Q G E R S A K G D A A
K P M L Y Y G X Y S E M S O D
```

20

3	5	1	6	4	8	7	9	2
6	2	9	1	7	5	8	3	4
8	4	7	9	2	3	1	6	5
7	3	2	5	1	9	4	8	6
4	8	5	7	3	6	2	1	9
1	9	6	4	8	2	5	7	3
2	6	3	8	5	1	9	4	7
9	1	4	2	6	7	3	5	8
5	7	8	3	9	4	6	2	1

19

21

DOCTOR	WARD
Dr. Francis	3
Dr. Gordon	2
Dr. Holmes	1
Dr. Inigo	4
Dr. James	5

22

V	I	R	G	I	N	I	A
E	U	R	Y	D	I	C	E
N	O	V	E	M	B	E	R
T	H	A	I	L	A	N	D
I	L	L	I	N	O	I	S
L	A	D	Y	B	I	R	D
A	L	A	C	A	R	T	E
T	U	R	M	E	R	I	C
O	V	E	R	B	I	T	E
R	A	S	P	U	T	I	N

Answer: Ventilator

23

C	U	B	E		F	A	N	C	I	E	S	T
H		I		E		G		O		N		O
I	N	T	E	N	S	E		U	S	H	E	R
L		E		T		N		N		A		E
D	I	S	C	R	E	D	I	T	I	N	G	
R			E		A		E		C		R
E	S	C	A	P	E		F	R	E	E	Z	E
N		O		R		P		A			A
	I	N	T	E	L	L	E	C	T	U	A	L
S		V		N		E		T		S		N
T	W	I	C	E		A	V	E	R	A	G	E
I		C		U		S		D		G		S
R	E	T	U	R	N	E	D		M	E	S	S

24

Cirrhosis = 4. LIVER

Nephritis = 1. KIDNEY

Glaucoma = 6. EYE

Asthma = 8. LUNGS

Myocarditis = 2. HEART

Lordosis = 3. SPINE

Anemia = 5. BLOOD

Gastritis = 7. STOMACH

25

C A L L E D
A S L E E P
P A S T E D
G L A S S Y
P A R K E D
E Q U I N E
C O R D O N
S E A S O N
S P O O N S
M E D I U M
M O N K E Y
C O T T O N
M A R T E N
W A T E R S
T A U G H T
H O N E S T

Answer: Let's run some tests

26

1.Target, 2. Tenth, 3. Waffle, 4. Atlas, 5. Grand, 6. Theirs.

27

Quote: "...their greatest strength and fatal flaw."

28

1.Urges, 2. Grouse, 3. Gnu, 4. Gorse, 5. Rouen, 6. Euro, 7. Rouge, 8. Snore, 9. Runes, 10. Senor.

29

(Crossword grid with words)

BLADDER
STOMACH
PANCREAS
KIDNEYS
TONSILS
LIVER
CAPILLARY
APPENDIX
INTESTINE
PITUITARY GLAND
VEIN
BRONKULUS
URETER
UTERUS
PHARYNX
LARYNX
WINDPIP
THYROID

31

```
S T C T Z B S W I M P C K F N
W Q D D S U N C W I O L P L T
R R W N R I D D W T S E U J S
D I K G U D T T R X T A I U I
H P E O G R I E W R B N Z V N
G O H P R N S E H J O E L C O
N W E I E H X E T T Y R O S I
P O R T E R I T N I S A O W T
T N A T L U S N O C C E W K P
N T D V T M P E B Y W I N A E
X S U L Q L G M O Q Y W A A C
N I A L P A H C I B S H G N E
P H Y S I C I A N L J G N S R
P T E R U F Z D M L O X Y E M
S B T X K M H E J M B F C D I
```

30

C	L	O	C	P	A	B	E	D	P
H	E	A	K	I	T	V	I	S	A
N	O	R	N	E	B	P	C	I	N
I	M	T	T	S	O	I	L	T	O
T	R	U	B	E	A	R	S	T	R
O	C	B	S	E	P	D	K	E	S
R	S	R	U	N	E	S	N	A	L
S	E	S	O	R	R	Y	N	E	B
D	O	C	T	S	S	A	I	C	I
L	U	N	C	H	T	R	M	E	D

ANSWERS: Clock, Patients, Bedpan, Visitors, Heart monitor, Clipboard, Blankets, Beepers, Scrubs, Nurses, Doctors, Lunch trays, Medicine.

32

	S	T	A	R	E		S	C	A	M	S
S		R		O		R		A		A	V
P	R	I	V	A	T	E		S	C	R	E E
A		P		R		P		T		R	R
C	A	S	H		C	R	E	A	T	I	N G
E			G		E		W		E		E
	U	N	D	E	R	S	T	A	N	D	S
S		U		N		E		Y			C
C	O	N	C	E	R	N	S		S	P	A R
O		N		R		T		A		I	A
O	P	E	R	A		E	X	C	I	T	E S
P		R		T		D		E		T	H
	T	Y	P	E	S		U	S	U	A	L

33

8	6	2	1	9	3	5	7	4
9	5	4	8	7	6	3	2	1
3	1	7	5	4	2	9	8	6
7	4	1	9	6	8	2	3	5
5	2	8	3	1	7	6	4	9
6	3	9	2	5	4	8	1	7
2	7	6	4	3	9	1	5	8
4	8	5	6	2	1	7	9	3
1	9	3	7	8	5	4	6	2

34

35

DOCTOR	FIELD
Kate	Surgery
Leonardo	Orthopedics
Micah	Pediatrics
Nathan	Anesthetics
Olive	Cardiologist

36

S	I	L	V	E	R
T	O	U	C	A	N
E	A	G	L	E	S
T	W	E	L	V	E
H	U	D	S	O	N
O	X	F	O	R	D
S	C	H	O	O	L
C	O	N	R	A	D
O	R	E	G	O	N
P	U	R	P	L	E
E	U	R	O	P	E

Answer: Stethoscope

37

There are 12 in total.

38

"I'm afraid we're still waiting on your test results, son, so you'll have to be a little patient!"

39

S T R E A M · S ·
M · E · · E A T S S
I S S U E D · A ·
L · E · L · I · T
E S T I M A T E D
· E · T · · I · A
· V · E D I T O R
T E A M · · A · E
· N · S A I N T S

40

P O W E R S
W H E N C E
L O W E S T
D A N C E R
S E C O N D
D I V O T S
S T O O P S
C H I M E D
A L W A Y S
I S L A N D
A S L A N T
C H U T E S
P O U N D S
O T T E R S
T H R I F T

Answer: WHERE DOES IT HURT

41

Chest = 4. STERNUM

Leg = 8. FEMUR

Knee = 3. PATELLA

Arm = 1. HUMERUS

Back = 7. VERTEBRA

Jaw = 6. MANDIBLE

Head = 2. CRANIUM

Foot = 5. TALUS

42

1.Lime, 2. Claimed, 3. Malice, 4. Decimal, 5. Mailed, 6. Decal, 7. Acid, 8. Camel, 9. Email, 10. Medial.

43

44

9	4	8	6	5	1	7	2	3
3	2	6	8	4	7	1	9	5
7	5	1	3	2	9	8	4	6
2	1	4	7	6	3	5	8	9
8	7	3	1	9	5	4	6	2
6	9	5	4	8	2	3	7	1
4	3	2	5	7	6	9	1	8
5	8	9	2	1	4	6	3	7
1	6	7	9	3	8	2	5	4

45

KID	FIRST AID ITEM
Brianna	Band Aid
Charles	Painkiller
David	Thermometer
Eduardo	Sling
Freya	Ointment

46

47

C	L	E	A	C	C	O	N	S	U
R	E	T	N	O	O	T	S	P	L
E	P	R	E	R	K	R	U	A	T
F	H	O	E	G	A	I	R	R	A
I	Y	P	N	U	P	E	G	A	N
W	S	E	S	R	H	O	E	M	T
D	I	O	A	P	A	N	D	I	C
I	M	T	R	I	R	M	A	C	I
O	R	H	E	S	T	G	A	R	S
T	C	O	D	R	E	N	E	D	T

ANSWERS: Cleaner, Cook, Consultant, Porter, Midwife, Physiotherapist, Triage nurse, Surgeon, Paramedic, Pharmacist, Doctor, Gardener.

48

N	I	G	E	R	I	A
E	L	E	C	T	R	A
B	E	L	G	I	U	M
U	N	K	N	O	W	N
L	E	O	N	A	R	D
I	T	A	L	I	A	N
Z	I	P	C	O	D	E
E	M	E	R	S	O	N
R	I	C	H	A	R	D

Answer: Nebulizer

49

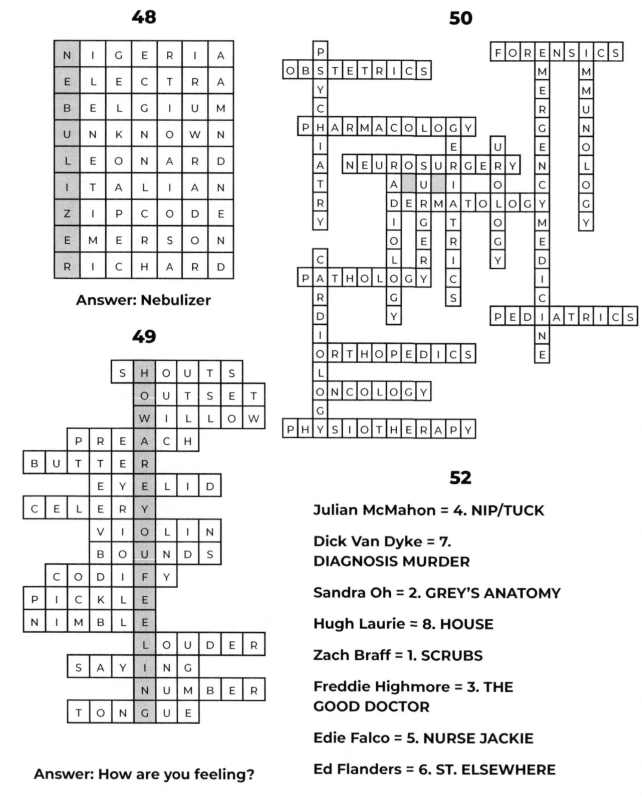

Answer: How are you feeling?

50

52

Julian McMahon = 4. NIP/TUCK

Dick Van Dyke = 7. DIAGNOSIS MURDER

Sandra Oh = 2. GREY'S ANATOMY

Hugh Laurie = 8. HOUSE

Zach Braff = 1. SCRUBS

Freddie Highmore = 3. THE GOOD DOCTOR

Edie Falco = 5. NURSE JACKIE

Ed Flanders = 6. ST. ELSEWHERE

53

1.Innate, 2. Tenant, 3. Taint, 4. Tine, 5. Patent, 6. Pint, 7. Tenpin, 8. Titian, 9. Nape, 10. Titan.

54

```
X O J J Z V Q R C O U E D R A
M D I P M Y E E X L S R E O U
V Q P D F T P Y T Y T U F T T
N G P N E C G R R S R S I A O
Y Y I M L E A I I F U S B L C
I E Y H N S N M E C G E R I L
W X A T O G X T R F F R I T A
O I A U E B F Q L Z L P L N V
V N N P P I R D V I O D L E E
K D U K S O E B Y P W O A V Y
W M E L T V X F P O M O T B E
P D C I S T E V W V E L O H P
I Q N D V J T U U U T B R L Z
U O Q C Q T Y A R X E N S H S
M R O T A B U C N I R X X F H
```

55

1.Beaver, 2. Angle, 3. Tapir, 4. Phi, 5. Dent. Quote: "Leaving better and happier."

57

7	4	2	3	1	5	9	6	8
3	5	8	2	6	9	4	1	7
1	6	9	7	8	4	3	5	2
6	1	4	9	3	7	2	8	5
8	2	5	1	4	6	7	3	9
9	7	3	5	2	8	6	4	1
2	8	6	4	9	1	5	7	3
4	3	7	8	5	2	1	9	6
5	9	1	6	7	3	8	2	4

58

59

PATIENT	LUNCH
Mr. Monroe	Cheese roll
Mr. Nesbit	Bean salad
Mr. O'Hara	Tuna sandwich
Mr. Peterson	Chicken soup
Mr. Quigley	Macaroni cheese
Mr. Reynolds	Hamburger

60

```
T H E S I S ▓ A
I ▓ X ▓ I N C H
R A T I N G ▓ T
E ▓ R ▓ H ▓ O ▓
D I A M E T E R S
▓ D ▓ E ▓ X ▓ O
▓ E A C T I O N
E A R N ▓ S ▓ A
▓ S ▓ S I S T E R
```

61

"Transplant nurses never go on dates, because they hate risking rejection!"

62

```
C A L L E D
      E A S T E R
    M A T T E R
T H I R D S
        S E A S O N
      B E D B U G
B U T T O N
        D O N K E Y
      S Y S T E M
B R O N C O
G A T E A U
        F O R A G E
        O U T P U T
    D A R K E N
        A R I S E N
P R I S O N
        C L A I M S
B A N A N A
        N A T T E R
```

ANSWER: "Let's send you for a scan"

128

63

O	M	A	H	A
X	E	N	O	N
Y	U	C	C	A
G	L	E	N	N
E	G	Y	P	T
N	O	R	T	H
M	U	S	I	C
A	P	R	I	L
S	A	R	A	H
K	A	F	K	A

Answer: Oxygen mask

65

U	X	H	N	U	C	B	T	W	U	I	U	I	D	S
Z	S	A	U	K	T	S	L	E	R	E	C	O	Z	R
O	K	N	Z	B	E	T	O	A	E	Q	O	U	C	E
F	R	D	R	R	K	Y	O	S	N	H	K	A	P	N
V	E	R	D	P	I	L	L	O	W	K	S	T	M	R
R	H	A	S	D	S	O	G	K	H	T	E	D	F	O
M	E	I	T	S	R	I	E	Z	E	Z	D	T	E	C
H	Z	L	S	T	E	A	O	R	L	L	R	K	Y	B
W	A	P	N	R	E	R	S	F	H	U	A	H	O	N
L	T	O	Q	L	A	T	T	Y	P	K	O	P	P	X
M	C	X	N	G	L	Y	Z	T	C	W	B	W	R	P
I	N	C	L	I	N	E	R	T	A	P	T	Z	L	G
H	V	V	W	J	H	B	K	E	T	M	O	R	K	I
G	F	X	S	Z	J	L	X	C	M	W	O	D	O	Z
E	K	A	R	B	Y	V	X	C	J	T	F	H	L	O

64

P	H	M	A	G	A	E	A	D	P
P	O	E	N	I	Z	H	N	O	H
U	N	N	O	V	E	L	E	S	C
Z	E	C	H	A	R	W	O	T	H
Z	L	E	B	O	G	E	L	S	A
S	P	H	O	O	E	R	H	S	N
N	G	O	T	K	H	B	S	E	G
A	R	A	P	H	T	R	U	H	E
C	K	S	H	P	O	O	O	T	O
W	A	T	C	E	N	T	L	C	F

ANSWERS: Phone charger, Magazine, Headphones, Puzzle book, Novel, Change of clothes, Towels, Snacks, Photograph, Watch, Pen, Toothbrush.

66

Largest blood vessel = 5. AORTA

Longest legbone = 1. FEMUR

Smallest bone = 2. STAPES

Longest nerve = 8. SCIATIC

Thinnest skin = 3. EYELIDS

Heaviest internal organ = 7. LIVER

Only body part without a blood supply = 4. CORNEA

Largest muscle = 6. GLUTEUS

67

PATIENT	BONE
Mrs. Robinson	Hip
Mrs. Sanchez	Toe
Mr. Thomas	Rib
Mr. Underwood	Leg
Mr. Vincent	Skull
Miss Williams	Wrist

68

5	1	9	3	4	8	7	2	6
6	8	2	7	1	9	3	4	5
4	7	3	5	2	6	9	8	1
1	3	6	9	5	4	8	7	2
2	9	8	1	7	3	6	5	4
7	4	5	6	8	2	1	9	3
8	2	1	4	6	7	5	3	9
9	6	7	2	3	5	4	1	8
3	5	4	8	9	1	2	6	7

69

70

1.Spinach, 2. Spain, 3. Chain, 4. China, 5. Panics, 6. Pain, 7. Spiny, 8. Pachisi, 9. Sync, 10. Spinachy.

71

1.Ecuador, 2. Hotmail, 3. Bears, 4. Thyme, 5. Tenet. Quote: "The beating heart of our medical system."

73

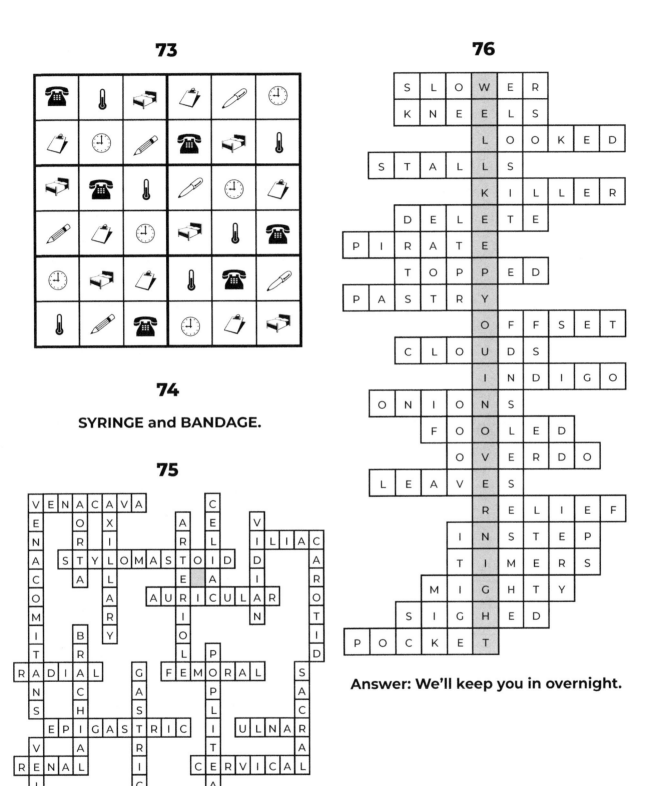

74

SYRINGE and BANDAGE.

75

```
V E N A C A V A       C
E     O   X       A R E         V
N     R   I     S T Y L O M A S T O I D   I L I A C
A   S T Y L O M A S T O I D   D       I L I A C
C     A   L     E   A   A U R I C U L A R   R
O     R   A         I O L       N       O
M     Y   R Y       O L   P             T
I       B         L   P             I
T       B R     G   F E M O R A L     D
R A D I A L     G A S   P L       S
N       C H     A S   P L I       A
S       H     S T R I C   U L N A R   A
  E P I G A S T R I C     I         A
V       A     R       T           A
R E N A L     I     C E R V I C A L
  E I N       C   I A             A
    N       S U B C L A V I A N
```

76

```
S L O W E R
K N E E L S
      L O O K E D
S T A L L S
      K I L L E R
  D E L E T E
P I R A T E
  T O P P E D
P A S T R Y
      O F F S E T
  C L O U D S
      I N D I G O
O N I O N S
  F O O L E D
  O V E R D O
L E A V E S
      R E L I E F
  I N S T E P
  T I M E R S
  M I G H T Y
  S I G H E D
P O C K E T
```

Answer: We'll keep you in overnight.

131

77

T	E	N	N	I	S
H	O	W	A	R	D
E	L	E	V	E	N
R	E	A	G	A	N
M	A	D	R	I	D
O	R	A	N	G	E
M	E	X	I	C	O
E	L	N	I	N	O
T	H	O	M	A	S
E	D	W	A	R	D
R	U	D	D	E	R

Answer: Thermometer

78

6	7	1	4	3	9	8	5	2
4	2	5	7	1	8	9	6	3
8	3	9	6	2	5	4	7	1
3	4	6	8	9	2	5	1	7
1	5	8	3	6	7	2	4	9
2	9	7	1	5	4	3	8	6
5	6	4	9	7	3	1	2	8
9	1	2	5	8	6	7	3	4
7	8	3	2	4	1	6	9	5

79

ROOM No.	NURSE
1	Brian
2	Freda
3	Ellie
4	Anne
5	David
6	Catherine

80

E	I	N	V	Y	H	Q	Q	S	Y	S	R	B	O		O
R	D	J	E	R	B	E	E	A	A	K	L	D	X		Y
U	Q	A	F	B	C	X	A	T	E	O	V	X	Y		X
T	B	S	E	J	E	V	U	R	O	E	M	S	G		I
A	H	U	P	L	V	R	A	D	T	E	G	P	E		Y
R	Z	E	F	W	A	X	P	W	M	R	E	O	N		T
E	C	E	I	T	I	R	N	E	K	Y	A	O	Q		I
P	R	G	I	G	E	M	G	I	U	Z	J	T	U		S
M	S	O	L	S	H	P	H	G	C	P	Y	Y	E		N
E	N	Z	S	A	W	T	W	H	B	G	P	Y	B		E
T	E	U	E	I	E	P	Y	T	D	O	O	L	B		D
W	R	M	E	T	A	B	O	L	I	C	R	A	T	E
E	E	T	A	R	G	N	I	H	T	A	E	R	B		N
S	S	E	N	S	U	O	I	C	S	N	O	C		L	O
B	O	D	Y	M	A	S	S	I	N	D	E	X		R	B

132

81

82

	C		F		V		S		A		T
N	A	M	E	S	A	K	E		S	O	U	R
	T		A		M		V		S		T
S	E	A	R		P	R	E	V	I	O	U	S
	G				I		R		S		
F	O	R	W	A	R	D		S	T	I	C	K
	R		I		E		P		E		O
C	Y	C	L	E		K	I	D	D	I	N	G
			D		S		C				S
B	U	L	L	E	T	I	N		P	A	I	N
	S		I		Y		I		L		D
B	E	E	F			L	E	C	T	U	R	E	S
	S		S		E		E		S		R

83

P	A	R	E	L	B	M	A	L	A
E	T	U	S	C	I	D	N	C	V
L	E	M	S	A	P	U	L	A	I
L	R	P	T	Y	O	I	D	S	C
A	L	E	E	H	L	L	U	K	L
F	V	I	R	N	U	M	C	O	E
I	B	S	M	E	R	U	S	C	C
L	U	H	U	U	I	D	A	R	Y
A	B	I	C	S	A	N	E	R	X
T	I	A	A	L	C	S	U	I	B

ANSWERS: Patella, Femur, Mandible, Clavicle, Scapula, Sternum, Pelvis, Hyoid, Skull, Fibula, Humerus, Coccyx, Tibia, Calcaneus, Radius, Rib.

84

1.Unable, 2. Ulna, 3. Clean, 4. Banal, 5. Manual, 6. Balance, 7. Manacle, 8. Becalm, 9. Albumen, 10. Unlace.

86

"No one listened to the doctor's advice about using an otoscope. It went in one ear and out the other."

87

S	█	D	█	O	█	M	A	D
L	E	A	R	N	█	E	█	A
U	█	N	█	C	L	A	I	M
R	O	G	U	E	█	S	█	E
█	█	E	█	█	█	U	█	█
S	█	R	█	N	U	R	S	E
T	R	O	V	E	█	I	█	L
O	█	U	█	A	P	N	E	A
P	O	S	E	R	█	G	█	N

89

CONSULTANT	DAY
Dr. Andrews	Wednesday
Dr. Blair	Tuesday
Dr. Chavez	Saturday
Dr. Dorfman	Friday
Dr. Ellis	Thursday
Dr. Farouk	Monday
Dr. Graham	Sunday

88

```
B O W L E D
      W O O D E N
        Y E A R L Y
      M O U N T S
        U N D O N E
        H E A L T H
      C A M E R A
        V I C T O R
R E F I N E
        C A B I N S
P E R S O N
S U N D A Y
        C A N N O T
    M U R A L S
        S L U D G E
      M E E K E R
        R O B U S T
    B R I D G E
        M I R A G E
    A N S W E R
A S S E S S
```

ANSWER: Do you have any allergies?

90

C	H	I	N	A
E	L	G	A	R
N	A	N	C	Y
T	E	X	A	S
R	I	S	E	R
I	N	D	I	A
F	U	D	G	E
U	N	C	L	E
G	R	E	E	K
E	L	L	E	N

Answer: Centrifuge

134

91

6	8	5	4	2	1	7	3	9
9	7	2	8	5	3	1	6	4
1	4	3	6	7	9	2	8	5
4	5	1	7	6	8	9	2	3
3	2	9	1	4	5	6	7	8
7	6	8	3	9	2	4	5	1
5	3	6	9	1	7	8	4	2
8	9	4	2	3	6	5	1	7
2	1	7	5	8	4	3	9	6

95

92

1.Golf, 2. Woody, 3. Fame, 4. Emu, 5. Teeth, 6. H.E.R. Quote: "Forget how you made them feel."

96

CHEESE SALAD

HAMBURGER

VEGETABLE STEW

CHOCOLATE ICECREAM

97

HEADACHE and DIZZINESS.

94

98

	S	C	E	N	T		R	I	V	E	R
A		A		O		A		N		M	S
D	E	V	I	O	U	S		D	R	O	O	P
A		E		N		S		U		T		I
P	U	S	H		Q	U	E	S	T	I	O	N
T			I		M			T		O		E
	T	R	A	N	S	P	A	R	E	N	T
M		E		F		T		Y				C
E	C	O	N	O	M	I	C		H	A	L	O
S		P		R		O		S		R		O
S	T	E	A	M		N	A	T	U	R	A	L
Y		N		A		S		A		A		S
	P	S	A	L	M		B	R	A	Y	S

99

M	U	S	C	L	Y
		B	O	O	K	E	D
			U	N	K	I	N	D
			C	H	E	A	T	S
			A	L	W	A	Y	S
C	O	U	P	O	N
P	I	N	I	N	G
			L	O	U	D	E	R
E	N	O	U	G	H
			S	O	U	N	D	S
			M	O	T	I	O	N
	C	R	E	E	P	S
		L	I	T	T	L	E
			C	O	M	E	D	Y
			D	E	C	E	N	T
C	E	L	L	A	R
			Y	O	N	D	E	R

ANSWER: You can go home tomorrow.

100

Islets of Langerhans = 3. PANCREAS

Alveoli = 8. LUNGS

Epidermis = 7. SKIN

Amygdala = 1. BRAIN

Gastric fundus = 2. STOMACH

Acetabulum = 4. PELVIS

Pulmonary valve = 5. HEART

Lingual papillae = 6. TONGUE

101

1. Meaner, 2. Ramen, 3. Tame, 4. Matter, 5. Marten, 6. Matte, 7. Meter, 8. Rename, 9. Natter, 10. Entreat.

103

P	A	R	K	R	E	S	T	A	U
C	G	N	I	R	E	S	S	E	R
H	L	O	T	D	S	H	O	R	A
A	H	A	I	R	O	C	W	E	N
P	G	A	R	D	N	V	S	R	T
E	L	G	Y	E	N	E	E	C	A
C	E	P	M	N	S	N	R	E	F
O	C	T	I	O	T	I	O	T	S
F	E	R	H	O	O	E	N	C	E
F	E	E	S	P	I	L	E	T	S

ANSWERS: Parking lot, Restaurant, Chapel, Hairdresser, Convenience store, Gardens, Showers, Café, Gym, Reception, Coffee shop, Toilets.

104

BOOKCASE
CREAMER
FRESHAIR
TELEVISION
MAGAZINES
CHEESE
NEWSPAPERS
NAP
SODA
FOOTSTOOL

MUSIC TEA
SANDWICHES
MILK
CUSHION
RESTS
RADIO
FRIENDS

106

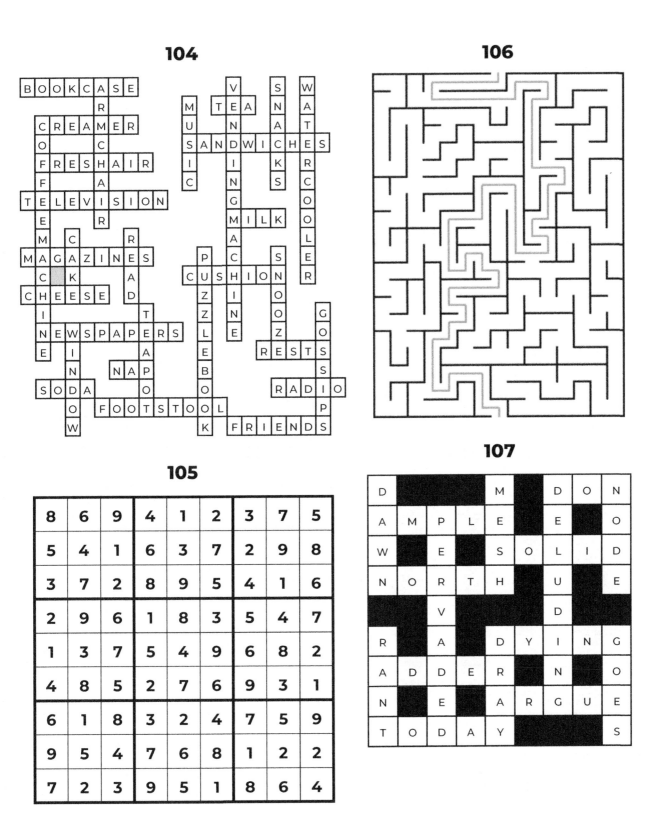

105

8	6	9	4	1	2	3	7	5
5	4	1	6	3	7	2	9	8
3	7	2	8	9	5	4	1	6
2	9	6	1	8	3	5	4	7
1	3	7	5	4	9	6	8	2
4	8	5	2	7	6	9	3	1
6	1	8	3	2	4	7	5	9
9	5	4	7	6	8	1	2	2
7	2	3	9	5	1	8	6	4

107

D				M		D	O	N
A	M	P	L	E		E		O
W		E		S	O	L	I	D
N	O	R	T	H		U		E
		V				D		
R		A		D	Y	I	N	G
A	D	D	E	R		N		O
N		E		A	R	G	U	E
T	O	D	A	Y				S

137

108

"Yes, I found that patient that I had lost. Ironically, he was in I.C.U."

109

```
O S T D J R H G G Y L G H T N
M E Q C W E A O C F L U W E W
M I O L T E N O J A G I R D K
I D G K R Z D D G S R D M C I
F L O W E R S B W Q L K H A H
T T S W Z J H Y Y I K O E N F
H H G S A O A E H K C Q I Y F
I T A N D N K C G O B E Z N S
C S B N I C E Y L Y T K A V E
M D D O K W S A T Z S H Z B E
Y N E B Q Y T R O P S N A R T
T E K P Y E O Z L V M G S U Y
R I C T S L A U N D R Y U J D
Z R A C L E A N S H E E T S M
R F P T T A O C D N A T A H I
```

110

SHELF	ITEM
1 (Top)	Sanitizer
2	Thermometer
3	Swabs
4	Gloves
5	Syringes
6	Bandages
7	Scissors
8 (Bottom)	Otoscope

111

A	D	E	L	E	I	D	E
U	L	T	I	M	A	T	E
T	H	A	N	A	T	O	S
O	K	L	A	H	O	M	A
C	A	N	A	D	I	A	N
L	A	U	G	H	I	N	G
A	L	P	A	C	I	N	O
V	I	C	T	O	R	I	A
E	I	N	S	T	E	I	N

112

D	I	P	S			E	L	L	I	P	S	I	S
E		O		S		E		N		E			O
C	H	O	I	C	E	S		T	I	M	E	D	
E		L		A		S		R		I			A
M	I	S	S	T	H	E	P	O	I	N	T		
B			T		N		D		A			E
E	N	T	R	E	E		Q	U	A	R	R	Y
R		R		R		K		C				E
	C	O	M	B	I	N	A	T	I	O	N	S
A		D		R		O		I		U		O
M	E	D	I	A		C	R	O	O	N	E	R
O		E		I		K		N		C		E
K	I	N	D	N	E	S	S		P	E	N	S

Printed in Great Britain
by Amazon

33972322R00077